A Quiet Strong Voice

A Voice of Hope amidst Depression, Anxiety, and Suicidal Thoughts

Dear Anu

You are not alone
You are loved
You belong
Hugs Lee ♡

Lee Horbachewski

BALBOA
PRESS

A DIVISION OF HAY HOUSE

Cover design by Ivan Terzic
Headshot Photography by Ilona Kohlmann
Editing by Denise Guichon and Natasha Tracy

Balboa Press books may be ordered through booksellers or by contacting:

Balboa Press
A Division of Hay House
1663 Liberty Drive
Bloomington, IN 47403
www.balboapress.com
1 (877) 407-4847

Printed in the United States of America.

ISBN: 978-1-4525-8862-9 (sc)
ISBN: 978-1-4525-8864-3 (hc)
ISBN: 978-1-4525-8863-6 (e)

Library of Congress Control Number: 2013922627

Balboa Press rev. date: 01/09/2014

Testimonials

Thank you so much, Lee, for sending copies of *A Quiet Strong Voice* to us for the Men at Risk program. I started reading it, and I couldn't put it down.

It is so inspiring to hear about the depths of your illness and how you worked on your recovery. It is a very hopeful, heartfelt story that will reach people who are suffering or who have been there in the past. You write so well that I could picture you in the settings you describe.

I also appreciate chapter 9 for the resources, making your book very practical for people to use. The other staff and executive director at SPRC are very impressed as well.

Barbara Campbell, RSW

Men at Risk program coordinator

Suicide Prevention Resource Centre, Grande Prairie, AB

Lee Horbachewski hits the mark by her honesty about all the emotions she was experiencing. Most importantly, she highlights the importance of acknowledging all emotions so that they can be seen and heard. I appreciated her vulnerability and believe this book is a valuable resource.

Tessa Burns

Registered psychologist and owner of Serenity Now Wellness Centre

Lee Horbachewski's book is a beacon of hope to those who are experiencing the darkness of depression, anxiety or thoughts of suicide. Those who are struggling and those who care for someone who is suffering will find inspiration, hope, and a wealth of resources in this book. With ruthless honesty and deep compassion for herself and others Lee shares her story and reminds us all of the choice to open again and again to learning and life.

Oriah Mountain Dreamer
Author of *The Invitation*

A profoundly helpful, heartfelt and authentic book by a brave and beautiful soul. An opus of overcoming! There are many books written about depression but very few cut to the heart of the matter like this one. Highly recommended!

Jeff Brown
Author of 'Soulshaping'.

Depression, anxiety, and *suicide* are not just words, but experiences that I'm all too familiar with. They have been a part of my life experience countless times. In my family alone, there have been five suicides (that I'm aware of), in three generations.

Mental Illness is on both sides of my family tree. My father had his own battles with darkness that led to a lot of substance abuse, countless suicide attempts, until he succeeded on November 19, 1984. I, too, have had my own struggles with darkness, depression, and anxiety. In my experience, it has been the anxiety that's even worse than the depression. But one feeds the other, and the vicious cycle begins by taking you on a spiraling isolating journey.

A *Quiet Strong Voice* is a necessary and helpful tool to remind us that we are not alone, that we are worthy, and that we matter! It gives us permission to ask for help, and to honor not only our light but also our darkness. It teaches us that we are worthy of love, especially our own.

The stigma of mental illness has been hidden, downplayed, and muted for far too long. My deepest thanks go out to Lee Horbachewski for sharing her truth and her vulnerability. Her commitment to see this book to completion is more than brave—it is pure love.

Natasja Fischer

Professional organizer and owner of Symmetry Works

Beautifully written, Lee's journey offers others hope, compassion, inspiration, and strength in a time when they need it the most. A *Quiet Strong Voice* ... an authentically moving book.

Charmaine Hammond

Bestselling author, *On Toby's Terms*

A *Quiet Strong Voice* is real, raw, and powerful. Lee's brutal honesty and her willingness to "tell all" offer an intense, insightful experience into the darkness that is depression, anxiety, and attempted suicide. There is a greater awareness and compassion that results when you journey through and share Lee's experience in each word that she has written. She has found her quiet strong voice; she is brave.

Jill Ethier

Owner/creator of
Unleash Your Greatness

A Quiet Strong Voice is a compelling piece of vulnerability, revealing the depths of despair, the dangers in depression, and the quicksand of suicide intention that can trap even the most beautiful, intelligent, and loving individuals.

Lee Horbachewski bravely exposes the truth of her torturous journey through anxiety, fear, depression, and multiple suicide attempts. Her intimate description of frantic attempts to end her life pull you into the story, enmeshing your emotions, heart, and longing for peace for this fragile woman.

Hope comes in opening hearts to others, to nature, and to our higher power, verifying that we can overcome disparaging, self-destructive, and depressive emotions.

Annette Stanwick

Award-winning author of *Forgiveness: The Mystery and the Miracle*

Lee has given us powerful insight into depression by sharing her journey. It is a must-read to ensure we are aware of the hidden symptoms of this life-threatening illness. You will relate to her pain and to her family's pain, and you will, most of all, understand the journey of recovery; you will cheer for her awakening out of the darkness. We all know someone with depression, and they deserve our understanding. When you read *A Quiet Strong Voice*, you will understand.

Melanie Hayden-Sparks
Founder and president
of Graduit Network

A Quiet Strong Voice speaks honestly and heart-fully to the desperate and seemingly hopeless battle of depression. Lee's journey is a true story that serves to illuminate all facets of her TRUTH: the compelling, intimate details of her illness and the unconditional love and support that she discovers, even in the most unexpected places, on her path to wellness. Lee's story serves as a bright light to the countless numbers of people, as well as to their families and loved ones, who are dealing with the dark and isolating effects of depression and anxiety.

Kari Dunlop
Founder/owner of Glinda Girls
and The Story Studio

I have never met someone so honest and open about her depression and attempted suicide. This story touched my heart in many ways, and every time an issue came up, I could feel Lee's pain and wanted nothing more than to grab her and to take her pain away. Suicide has affected so many people, and the person who commits suicide doesn't realize how devastating it is for everyone around them, or that there is hope. I am so honored and humbled to have Lee in my life and couldn't imagine life without her! *A Quiet Strong Voice* is a *must-read* for anyone who has even a whiff of depression or mental health challenges. Lee, you are the bravest woman I know!

Kelly Falardeau

Author of *No Risk No Rewards*

Every so often, someone will come along and gift you with the raw, honest, revelation of their experience. When this happens, you are changed forever. *A Quiet Strong Voice* is that gift. Lee Horbachewski helps to increase our understanding of mental illness and brings forth a tremendous offering of tools in which one can begin to hear their own quiet strong voice emerging. This is a gift to be shared.

Farhana Dhalla

International #1 best-selling author of *Thank You for Leaving Me*

A Quiet Strong Voice, Lee takes you through her journey of what was her reality, battling a dark war against depression and suicide, coming out on top. This book is sure to inspire anyone to be more open and aware to the disease of depression. If you do not understand the severe impact that depression can have on someone's life, you will after reading this beautiful piece.

Shelley Streit

Author of *Beyond the Rear-View Mirror*

Contents

Foreword xv

Poem: A Quiet Strong Voice xvii

Introduction xxi

Chapter 1   Denial: What Am I Pretending
              Not to Know? 1

    Living a Lie 6

    Christmas in Australia 9

    What I Know Now That I Didn't Know Then 12

Chapter 2   Awareness: Facing the Truth 13

    Darkness Overtakes 15

    Weaker and Weaker 18

    Entering a Foreign World 21

    I Want the Pain to End 30

    What I Know Now That I Didn't Know Then 36

Chapter 3   Acceptance: Surrendering
              and Letting Go 37

    Finding Lee 40

    Going Home 43

What I Know Now That I Didn't Know Then.............. 47

Chapter 4   Action: Taking Baby Steps...................... 48

    Boundaries...50

    Building a Support Network....................................57

    Embracing Anger 61

    Resilience 65

    Connection...68

    What I Know Now That I Didn't Know Then.............. 71

Chapter 5   Back to Reality.....................................72

    Learning to Be Open, Honest, and Vulnerable....... 75

    What I Know Now That I Didn't Know Then.............80

Chapter 6   Living Life... 81

    Present Tense 81

Chapter 7   Your Personal Reflection 85

    Facts 87

    Warning Signs 88

    Personal Reflection 91

    Stand Up for Yourself: Creating Healthy
        Boundaries 95

    Speak Up and Ask for Help: Creating Your
        Emotional Health Plan...97

    Emotional Health Plan Example.............................. 100

    Show Up with Kindness, Love, and
        Gratitude: Embracing All Emotions.................. 101

Chapter 8   Supporting a Loved One 103

Chapter 9   Resources and Help 109

   24-Hour Crisis Support Lines 109

   Global Resources 109

   Canadian Resources 111

   US Resources 112

   Australian Resources 112

   UK Resources 113

   Internet Resources 114

   Books That Have Inspired Me 114

   Books Specific to Mental Health 117

Gratitude 119

About the Author 123

Foreword

The relevance of this book is staggering. Depression and anxiety are on the rise, and there is a greater need for practical wisdom and helpful tools. It is in sharing our stories that others come to see that they are not alone. It takes courage to tell our deeply personal stories of pain.

Enter Lee Horbachewski.

Lee's courage is infectious. She inspired me to share my own story of darkness and suffering, a story I never thought I would share with the world. Lee helped me to see the truth: it is in sharing our stories that we can really begin to change the world in a meaningful way.

The book you are holding in your hands may change your life. It changed mine.

The change began when I first met Lee years ago. Immediately I was struck by her tremendous courage and kindness. Looking into her eyes, I could see the depths of pain she had experienced and the profound transformation that had followed. Her book is written beautifully and is an authentic portrayal of her journey from darkness into light and from suffering and struggle into insight and awareness.

A Quiet Strong Voice is a deeply personal and engaging story; it is a toolbox of practical and helpful tools, and it is a reservoir of peace and inspiration.

Lee describes in delicious detail the tools and strategies she used to move down the healing path of denial, awareness, acceptance, and action. She pours her soul into the pages. Her insights dazzle, and her compassion soothes.

Quite simply, Lee gets it. She gets the journey of moving through depression, anxiety, and attempted suicide. She gets the frustration of being in a system that was not helping her. She gets the intense need for self-awareness and self-love. And, she shares it with the world.

The benefits of hearing the real-life experience of someone who has struggled through depression and anxiety are undeniable. Hearing about the journey from someone who is open, real, self-aware, and courageous can be tremendously healing.

I have witnessed many people travel the dark and painful path of mental illness, and I have traveled that path myself. If you are struggling with mental illness, what I know for sure is that there is not one simple solution. Your solution will be a mosaic composed of different pieces that you will glue together based on what feels good to your heart. This book feels good to my heart, and I hope it will feel good to your heart too.

My wish for you is this: *may Lee's quiet strong voice be a source of comfort, hope, and strength.* I know it was for me.

All my love,

Gemma Stone

Registered psychologist,
author, and speaker

Poem: A Quiet Strong Voice

What if you feel all alone in the world—desperate, hopeless, and feeling isolated from all around you?

How would you cope; who could you turn to?

A quiet strong voice says, "Reaching out and asking for help is a sign of strength."

What if you feel there is no way out of your painful existence, thinking that everyone else is better off without you?

How could you find a glimmer of hope and faith?

A quiet strong voice says, "You are loved; this too shall pass."

What if you lie in bed at night, filled with anxiety, wondering if you will get any sleep, worrying whether or not you would wake numerous times throughout the night?

How would you calm yourself and relax into a restful slumber?

A quiet strong voice says, "Close your eyes, relax your body, and focus on your breath."

What if your heart feels like it is about to explode through your chest, your breathing is erratic, and fear is taking over your entire being?

How would you handle it?

A quiet strong voice says, "Breathe, close your eyes, and quiet your mind; this too shall pass."

What if becoming aware of how ill you are is the key to moving bravely forward with courage and resilience that you thought you never had?

How would you feel?

A quiet strong voice says, "You are much stronger than you think."

What if you accepted that you are not alone and many others have traveled through this painful journey and many are willing and able to support you?

Would that give you hope?

A quiet strong voice says, "You are not alone, and you belong."

What if you looked at the action to getting better as baby steps, giving yourself the permission to find happiness again in small stages?

Would that make things a little easier?

A quiet strong voice says, "You can get through this one minute at a time."

What if you have a loved one dealing with mental illness and you released yourself of responsibility, accepting that you cannot fix them, yet being there to love them unconditionally with unwavering acceptance and support?

How would that affect you?

> *A quiet strong voice says, "You are accepting, loving, compassionate, and kind."*

What would you say if I shared with you, "You *will* be okay! Although you may not see it right now, there is light at the end of the tunnel. You have strength within that you may not see, but it *is* there and you *will* get through this."

How do I know?

> *I listened to the quiet strong voice once I accepted that I have a disease called depression. I have been there in the darkness, isolation, helplessness, and hopelessness of depression, anxiety, and attempted suicide. I am grateful that I chose life and that I am here today.*

Introduction

This book is my raw, vulnerable and deeply personal journey through major depression, panic disorder and multiple suicide attempts. It is also a wealth of tools, resources and support to help people understand the depths of this dark and lonely place, and move onwards and upwards through both depression and anxiety.

What I want you to know is, depression and anxiety are real. This book is intended for both people suffering with this, and for people who are watching a loved one suffer through this. There are literally millions of people across the globe that have experienced the darkness, and have gone on to survive and thrive. There are people that can help you, and you need to connect with them. I know there is a lack of public education, and a stigma attached to mental illness – the challenge is, not to let that stand in the way of getting the help you or your loved one needs.

I made the choice to live, and this necessitated that I choose to grow while in discomfort and pain. Every day, I choose to commit to my mental health, and do whatever it takes not to go back into the dark and lonely place again. Everyone has this ability within them to make this choice.

When I was hospitalized in a psychiatric ward in 2004, I felt frustrated by the books my psychiatrist kept suggesting I read from the hospital library. They were thick books, small font and all written by doctors, psychiatrists or phD's. I longed to read something that I could relate to, something that didn't spiral me into a heavier sense of overwhelm. This book is intentionally kept short, the font is intentionally larger than normal, for that very reason.

I want to reiterate, as I do throughout this book, that there are people willing and able to help you. Without the professional help I received, I am certain I would not be here today. Many people do not reach out for help in fear of being judged, or thought of as crazy, psycho or a nut case. There is absolutely no shame in reaching out and in receiving help. In truth, it is a sign of strength, awareness, and wisdom within you.

Chapter 1

Denial: What Am I Pretending Not to Know?

Not everything that is faced can be changed,
but nothing can be changed until it is faced.

—James Baldwin

Early on a crisp, beautiful morning in July 2003, we arrive at the hospital. The nurse goes in search of a doctor as she sends Neil to the admitting desk. Here I am, now in the delivery room awaiting the arrival of our second daughter. I am alone when a seven-minute contraction attacks ferociously. I attempt to climb up onto the bed, but I can't do it. I move from surface to surface, trying everything I can think of to survive the excruciating pain. I can't even muster an audible voice; under my breath, I am asking for someone, for anyone, to help me. All at once Neil, the nurse, and the doctor enter the room and discover that the unusually long contraction has increased dilation from two centimeters to ten centimeters and that our daughter is ready to enter the world.

1

In less than forty-five minutes after we enter the hospital, our precious little girl is born. I had envisioned a peaceful beginning, holding her in my arms and sharing with Neil the magical first moments. This was something we had missed with the birth of our first daughter, who had been born six weeks prematurely and had been whisked off to an incubator immediately. But again, it was not to be. Suddenly, the quiet and isolated room becomes a flurry of activity; our little girl has a large growth on the back of her leg, and the nurses and doctors surround her. After only a brief moment of holding her in my arms, I must surrender her to be whisked away too.

Neil and I have no idea what the growth is, what could possibly be wrong with our precious little angel. We must wait until the early afternoon to receive some answers. As the pediatrician places our daughter stomach-down on the palm of his hand so that he can examine the growth, I notice that her skin is turning a dark shade of purple. My heart is pounding as I cry with panic, "She's stopped breathing!"

The doctor continues to examine the growth and once again, but with heightened panic, I scream at him, "She's stopped breathing! *Do something!*" Then the doctor rushes from the room with her. Neil and I follow closely behind. In a sterile room, as the doctor holds her in his hands, he suctions the mucus from her mouth, and thankfully, she begins to breathe once again.

After this initial scare, we don't feel quite as worried about the lump on her leg, though we are eager to find out what it is. After several anxious hours of waiting, finally we are given an explanation. We are told it is a congenital hemangioma, which is a raised birthmark that had grown in the womb. It will begin to shrink. Knowing it is nothing serious, Neil and I are at last able to fully enjoy the tiny miracle in our arms.

Twenty hours later, we are making our way home with our bundle of joy. Within the next couple of days, I realize that I am experiencing the same difficulties with breastfeeding this new baby as I did with my first daughter. I am overwhelmed by a deep sadness as I recognize that I will be unable, once again, to breastfeed because my milk ducts have plugged, presenting the possibility of a repeat of excruciating mastitis. I decide that this time I will not subject my starving baby or myself to numerous attempts, remedies, and unrelenting guilt talk from the public health nurse. I have surrendered to the knowledge that I will never know the deep pleasure of breastfeeding. My disappointment is replaced immediately with pride and joy as I watch my four-year-old daughter feed her little sister with care, sensitivity, and gentleness.

Although life in the first couple of weeks has been filled with sleepless nights, it has also been filled with joy, pride, and happiness as I take care of our beautiful girls. Then, one morning, I wake up and begin to cry for no apparent reason. The joy and pride are replaced by a deep, ineffable sadness that consumes me. The simplest of tasks, such as taking a shower, making breakfast, or changing a diaper, come to feel like an unbearable burden. My energy level is radically low, leaving me deeply fatigued and extremely short-tempered, abrupt, and impatient. "What the hell is going on?" I ask myself out loud. "I was absolutely fine yesterday, and now this?"

I am confused by the abrupt and inexplicable arrival of such emotion. Then, within a couple of hours, I am back to being my normal self, so I shrug it off as though it is nothing more than new-baby sleep deprivation. I tell myself I am just tired. The "sadness" pops up again, though, randomly, with absolutely no rhyme or reason and with greater frequency. One minute, I am as happy as can be, playing joyfully with my girls, and the next minute, the tears begin to flow uncontrollably. I am terribly confused, and I am beginning to worry about these episodes.

When Neil comes home from work, he asks, "How was your day?" and I can see that he is excited to be home with his girls. At the same time, he is exhausted from getting up with the baby throughout the night so that I can sleep and then getting up early for a full day of work.

"It was okay," I respond, and then I quickly hand off the girls to him so I can disappear into the silence of our bedroom, closing the door and retreating to solace and peace.

With the increase in the number of outbursts, I begin to feel some new emotions: frustration, anger, shame, and guilt. I feel agitated and begin to take it out on Neil, often saying to him, "You have no idea how lucky you are; you can just escape to work and be with adults and have a break."

Unreasonably, I view Neil's work as taking him away from the girls and me. Resentment builds within me as he continues to say no to my requests that he come home early in the afternoons. I begin to see his work as a threat; feelings of abandonment surface because he chooses work over us. As soon as my resentment takes hold, I am filled with shame and guilt.

"I am so sorry," I say as I break down in tears and fall into his arms. "You are such an incredible husband and father. I am truly blessed to have you. I'm just tired."

Finally, the wake-up call comes, and I know something serious is wrong with me. It is the day before my brother-in-law's wedding. Neil and his two brothers are relaxing in our hot tub. They are chatting, laughing, and celebrating, completely unaware that my head feels as though it will explode, my breathing is growing erratic, and I am feeling thoroughly overwhelmed. The baby is crying, and my other daughter is crying for my attention too. I think to myself, *I can't handle this; I am going to snap!* I lay the baby on the floor and storm out ferociously to where the men are, screaming and yelling that I cannot handle all of this by myself. "I'm leaving!" I tell them.

I snatch the keys and get behind the wheel of the car, tears streaming down my face. I floor the accelerator, sending gravel and dirt everywhere, and begin to drive recklessly at speeds of up to 180 kilometers per hour, not knowing where I am going or what I am doing. I go into town and buy a package of cigarettes even though I have quit smoking. I sit by the river and smoke the entire pack while trying to make sense of what has just happened.

Eventually, I return home to an extremely worried Neil who has no idea what has caused my outburst or where I had gone. He is relieved, but he is also very angry with me. Like me, he is confused, scared, and worried. That is enough for both of us to sit down and talk about what I have been feeling and experiencing.

"Honey, I can't explain it," I tell him. "One minute I'm fine, and then the next minute, I feel as if the world is over and that all hell is going to break loose. I feel like I no longer exist, that my life is now diapers, bottles, crying, and no sleep. Then I have moments of sheer bliss and joy. I don't know what is wrong with me," I say, feeling a sense of desperation.

Neil doesn't know what's wrong either and seems even more confused than before. "I just don't know how I can help you," he says. "I get up in the middle of the night. I come home and take care of the girls. I help you clean. I don't know what more I can do," he tells me in a desperate attempt to express his own frustration. "Why don't we see if Marie can look after the girls twice a week?" he suggests.

With sheer gratitude and relief, I agree to his suggestion. I feel some hope and have a vision of much-needed time to myself while knowing the girls will be looked after lovingly by Marie, who has taken care of our older daughter in the past.

As I lie in bed, I think to myself, *This is stupid; I am crazy, and I need to realize how lucky I am—quit it!* I determine that no matter what, I will not cause Neil any more pain and frustration. I will make the most of the days the girls are at Marie's; I will exercise, get together with my girlfriends, and take time for myself.

Living a Lie

For the next couple of months, I am angry with myself each time I feel the emotions welling. I beat them back down, telling myself, *Everything is okay. You can get through this; stop being weak and pathetic!* I continually suppress my emotions, not wanting them to surface in front of anyone, not even Neil. I don a mask of bravery for Neil and the girls, hiding my tears, fear, sadness, and loneliness. I am now plagued by these emotions, and on the two days a week that the girls spend with Marie, I lie in bed and cry all morning, working like a madwoman all afternoon to clean the house. I learn that keeping myself busy and allowing no distractions actually proves helpful in taming the outbursts.

But … My life is a lie.

In the eyes of others, I am the perfect mother and wife blessed with a blissful life. Indeed, I have an incredibly supportive and loving husband and two beautiful daughters. I could not ask for a more placid and content baby, and my older daughter dotes on her little sister; she is always eager to help me in any way she can. Yet, in spite of how wonderful my life is, in spite of the extraordinary support I receive, the darkness within me continues to grow and I continue to suppress it, hide it, and ignore it.

It is now October 2003. As I continue with my charade, I begin to feel the impact physically. Skipping breakfast and then filling myself with pop and other unhealthful foods has become the norm. Dinner is the only healthful meal I seem to eat, only because my family is all together. I expend so much energy suppressing my emotions, and I am so derailed by a poor diet, that I am becoming increasingly exhausted.

On this particular afternoon, I begin to feel nauseous. The very thought of food makes me gag, so I lie down on my bed. Little black circles appear before my eyes, and I feel light-headed and faint. "Just lie down and rest. This will pass," I tell myself.

Then suddenly, and for no apparent reason, my breathing becomes labored. I feel as though I am suffocating. First my breaths are rapid, then strained, and then I am short of breath. This occurs again and again like a yo-yo. I am sure that my heart is going to jump out of my chest. The pain is insufferable, and I am paralyzed with fear. The only thing I can manage to do is to wrap myself into the fetal position like a terrified child, sobbing.

"I am dying! I know it!" I call 9-1-1. The operator stays on the phone with me until the paramedics arrive and take me to the hospital.

After what feels like an eternity, a doctor finally gives me a diagnosis. I am suffering from exhaustion and dehydration, and it is possible I experienced a panic attack. Because of the extreme dehydration, I am admitted to the hospital and given IV nourishment. Throughout my stay in hospital, I remain in a drug-induced sleep, free of any and all responsibility. On the third day, I am sent home with a prescription for antianxiety medication to help me sleep and with a follow-up appointment with the doctor for the following week.

The antianxiety medication mercifully is helping me to sleep at night, which is of immense benefit. Waking rested each morning makes a wonderful difference. For the following two weeks, by the time I wake, Neil has already taken the girls to Marie's on his way to work. Thankfully, Marie has agreed to take care of the girls full-time until I feel strong enough to resume our two-day-a-week arrangement. I feel I have permission, especially from myself and a worried Neil, to take it easy and to rest.

What a difference these two weeks make. With the combination of the girls going to Marie's two days a week once more, weekly visits with the doctor, the antianxiety medication, and Neil's watchful, loving eye, I am feeling much stronger. The crying spells do not occur as often, and overall I seem to be coping well. I am filled with a renewed joy for life, feeling more in control of my emotions every day. The "lie" has been replaced by desire, love, and playfulness as I embrace the roles of mother and wife with more passion and purpose.

Christmas in Australia

Every couple of years, we spend Christmas in Australia with my family. This year I am looking forward to the trip with particular enthusiasm because everyone will meet our newest little girl. Selfishly, I am looking forward to receiving some help and support as well. Neil has only three weeks of vacation time, so we decide that the girls and I will leave three weeks ahead of him to give us more time to spend with my family.

Fortunately, both girls prove to be phenomenal fliers. My four-year-old keeps herself occupied with Play-Doh, coloring, watching movies, and even sleeping for a major portion of the flight from Hawaii to Sydney. My baby, now five months old, is amazingly calm and easy and sleeps a good deal too. This must be an unusual occurrence, because when the flight crew asks me, repeatedly, if I have drugged my children and I say no, they respond with disbelief.

My mum, dad, sister, brother-in-law, and nephew are waiting eagerly for us when we arrive, showering the girls with unbridled love and attention. I am relieved. I did it; I managed to travel calmly and successfully for twenty-four hours on my own with two children. Now I can relax and enjoy myself. I am filled with joy as I watch the love and affection unfolding before me, and I'm grateful to see my family.

Mum and Dad have a beautiful acreage about an hour and a half southwest of Sydney. Their property is surrounded by majestic one-hundred-year-old gum trees, as well as by other native trees and brush, and is separated from the neighboring property by a creek. I love to come here to enjoy the nature all around. My older daughter is entranced by the variety of different bugs, and it takes little persuading for her to go on a walk with Nanny to catch specimens in the new bug catcher that Nanny and Poppy bought for her. It is very peaceful here, and yet, it does not take long for me to remember how remote it is too.

Sadly, after a couple of days, Mum must return to work, and Dad, who has his own business, must work too. My vision of having daily help and support with the girls evaporates, and I begin to feel resentful that they are at work and not around the house to help me during the day. I feel isolated and removed from everything and everyone. I miss Neil tremendously and am longing for his support in helping with the nighttime feedings and with getting the girls up and out twice a week so that I can sleep in and have time to myself.

By the second week, my resentment has become frustration and anger. I realize I must talk to Mum and Dad before I go mad. I wait for what I believe is the perfect moment: Saturday morning, when Mum and Dad are having their tea and toast and reading the newspaper on the porch.

I am emphatic: "Mum, Dad, I came here early ahead of Neil, in hopes that you would be able to help me out with the girls. With both of you working and not being able to help me during the night, I am having a really tough time."

My mum and dad raised my sister, my brother, and me all alone with little to no help and with little to no money. My cry for help simply does not make sense to them.

"I don't understand why you need so much 'me' time. We had no one to help us. Your mum gets up at 5:00 a.m., and I work a full day. We can't give you what you need. We need to earn a living," says my dad.

How can I argue with that? Mum and Dad work hard. The last thing they need is to be looking out for me. An uncomfortable silence develops among us, and it begins to eat at my insides.

Thankfully, I go to stay with my sister and brother-in-law for a couple of days. They help me with the girls and keep my younger daughter in bed with them so they can feed her during the night. By the time Neil arrives on Christmas Day, I am out of my routine and am consumed with self-pity. I have forgotten, repeatedly, to take my antianxiety medication and have been reduced, once again, to sleepless nights and crying spells. By the time I return home to Calgary, I have effectively weaned myself from the medication within a short six-week time frame.[1] I tell myself that now that I am off the medication, I might as well stay off it.

With renewed gratitude for Neil's support and for the two days a week that the girls spend at Marie's, I am thinking, *I don't really need to take the medication. I am all over that stuff.* My seven-month-old is sleeping through the night now. I seem to be getting the rest I need, and gradually, I am creating a routine that seems to be working for me.

---

[1] **Note:** This is something that must *never* be done. Weaning off any prescribed antidepressant or antianxiety medication *must* be done under the supervision of a doctor.

What I Know Now That I Didn't Know Then

- I was pretending not to know I had postpartum depression.

- Lack of knowledge and awareness about postpartum depression held me back from receiving the professional help I needed.

- I need to be open and honest about how I am truly feeling.

- I need to be compassionate, kind, and forgiving toward myself.

- Living a lie does not serve anyone, especially me.

- Perceived "negative" emotions such as anger and frustration are not to be feared; they are part of human nature and are for us to experience. How I choose to react to them determines whether I have a healthy or an unhealthy response.

- I had a lack of knowledge about the triggers and signs of an anxiety attack and the tools to move through one.

- *Never* wean myself off medication without direct supervision from my doctor.

Chapter 2

Awareness: Facing the Truth

People grow through experience if they
meet life honestly and courageously.
—Eleanor Roosevelt

Neil and I begin to discuss whether or not I should go back to work. I am torn between my desire to stay home with my girls and my need for regular interaction with other adults. I realize I am fortunate to have the choice. The inner conflict of contemplating and weighing the advantages and disadvantages of each keeps my mind busy. Then I have an "aha" moment: I will go back to being a flight attendant on a casual basis, covering shifts when I am needed. I've been with the airline for eight years, so there shouldn't be a problem. Neil and I discuss this alternative and agree that it is a win–win solution. Feeling content, I make the most of the last couple of months of my maternity leave.

A couple of weeks prior to the end of my maternity leave, I go to the airline office to speak with management about my idea, thinking they will be happy to accommodate me. Much to my shock and dismay, however, I am told that choice is no longer available.

With a feeling of desperation I ask, "Can't you make an exception for me? After all, I've been with the airline almost since day one."

The response is typical: "If we do this for you, then we will have to do it for others, and we just can't do it."

Back to the drawing board. Do I go back to work or not? If I was to consider being a part-time flight attendant, I would be away from home for a minimum of eight nights each month, sometimes up to five days at a time. When I put it into perspective, my decision is an easy one. I am not willing to be away from my family for that much time, nor am I willing to work in the office from Monday to Friday. Seeing my daughters for only two hours each evening is not acceptable to me.

It is July 2004, and my maternity leave has ended. My decision not to return to work is one of the most difficult choices I have had to make. I am filled with many and varied emotions: joy at being able to spend time with my girls, relief that I will no longer have to work crazy hours, fear of the unknown, and grief over the loss of an eight-year career that I worked hard to create. I go back to the office to return all the company property I had in my possession and to pick up my belongings. I am shocked at the lack of response to my leaving. Nobody thanks me for my service to the organization; there is no good-bye party, no parting gift—nothing. I have spent eight years of my life dedicated to this airline, and nobody seems to care. I am overcome with sadness and anger as I leave the office, and I cry all the way home.

There is no way I could have predicted the anger I am feeling, the deep sense that I have been used and then discarded like a piece of garbage. I am consumed with "What if?" with "How could they?" and with "Who do they think they are?" The frustration and resentment builds.

As weeks pass, I find that I am lashing out and getting angry over petty things. A simple, "Mom, can I ...?" drives me into a fit. When Neil asks, "What did you do today?" I fly into a defensive outburst. Once again, for no apparent reason, I am beginning to have sudden crying spells. I am caught up in the belief that my identity is gone, and in turn, I resent having children. Again I am resentful of Neil going to work and leaving everything behind for me. Right now I identify myself with cleaning the house, feeding kids, doing laundry, and making dinner. I am living an existence filled with taking care of everyone else but me. I am beginning to skip meals, I stop showering regularly, and I am waking in the middle of the night.

Darkness is overtaking me. Unaware of what is happening, I continue to pretend not to know the depths of what I later discover to be depression. I am not even aware that is what is wrong. I continue to wear a mask: the supermom, the devoted wife, the people pleaser. I keep busy by cleaning, tidying, and doing whatever else I can do to attempt to bring myself some sanity. Yet in the darkness of wakeful nights, I am consumed by fear, doubt, and unknowing.

Darkness Overtakes

The sleepless nights are becoming unbearable for me. I am filled with dread as I lay my head on the pillow, knowing that I will wake at 1:30 a.m., then at 3:15 a.m., then at 4:30 a.m., almost like clockwork, every single night. I am using every ounce of my energy just to take care of my girls. All I want to do is sleep the day away. On the days that my younger daughter goes to Marie's, I wait in fear for my kindergartner to get home.

I lie in the front entry, curled in the fetal position, filled with anxiety, knowing that I simply cannot fulfill the important task of being a mom. I feel so guilty that in those first moments when she arrives home from school, I am unable to provide her with emotional stability. I am unable to provide her with a mother who can sit with her and talk about her day, a mother who can simply be present. I believe she deserves better than what I have to give her right now. I believe I am scarring her for life because I cannot provide her with what she needs at five years old. I believe I am ruining her life and that she must go to school each day saying, "Mommy is always crying, yelling, and screaming." I think to myself, *How can I be like this with my own child? What is wrong with me?*

Friends and family are beginning to see the signs of my "condition," which are becoming increasingly difficult to conceal. Every time someone says to me, "Just snap out of it," I feel frustrated and angry. I think to myself, *I wish I could just snap out of it. Do you really think I want to be like this? Just shut up and leave me alone!* Now the pattern of withdrawing from people is recurring.

I know I am getting worse, yet still I deny it. I wish and wait for the day that I will "snap out of it." I know that I cannot continue like this; it is all so hopeless. I just don't know what to do. My everyday life is overwhelmed with despair, helplessness, hopelessness, isolation, fear, and desperation. I wonder, "What is the point of going on?" I think everyone else would be better off without me. I am causing Neil and our girls so much pain, and they don't deserve any of it.

I begin searching for answers and doing research on the Internet about various illnesses. I turn to holistic treatments such as cranial sacral therapy and holistic medicines. In desperation, I attend a health expo and am drawn to a booth for the Inside Out Leadership Development Group. I am greeted by two of the warmest people I have met in a very long time. I feel at ease with them instantly, particularly with the man. I ask them if they know of a good clairvoyant, a form of help I have never tried. They point me in the right direction.

As I listen to the clairvoyant, uneasiness sweeps over me. Among other things, she tells me, "If you do not treat your depression, you will die!"

"Depression—I don't have depression," I tell myself, and yet, there is a nagging knot in my stomach. I feel as though I will vomit; I am shaking like a leaf, and I am consumed by weird emotions. After the session ends, I feel even more lost. I am drawn back to the first booth, and fortunately the man, Wayne, is still there.

"How did your session go?" he asks me, with genuine interest.

I break down into uncontrollable sobbing and fall into his arms. With pure acceptance, this stranger holds me and allows me to cry. I am unable to speak; I just need to be held and comforted. After a few moments, which feel like eternity, I calm down. I have a strong instinct that I must sign up for the Connections Retreat that is scheduled for November.

"Wayne, will you be there?" I ask him.

"Would you like me to be there?" he asks.

"Yes, I would," I reply with desperate eagerness.

"Then yes, I will be," Wayne replies, and in that moment, I am comforted.

Weaker and Weaker

> I've never tried to block out the memories of the past, even though some are painful. Everything you live through helps to make you the person you are now.
>
> —Sophia Loren

The nausea I have been experiencing has begun to cause me to vomit every morning. I am becoming weaker and weaker each day. I am still not sleeping at night. On many occasions, my neighbor and friend, Leslie, comes to check on me after a worried phone call from Neil because I am having difficulty breathing. Each time Leslie comes over, she sees me at my most vulnerable: naked, sobbing uncontrollably, and in a serious state of panic. With each of her visits, I am allowed some relief as she manages to calm me enough so that I can relax and sleep.

I am having weekly visits with my doctor and am losing an average of eight pounds per week. In a four-week period, I have lost almost 40 pounds, weighing a mere 110 pounds on my five-foot-eight-inch frame. No one knows what is wrong with me. I am sent for a gastrointestinal test to ascertain whether there are any blockages in my stomach, and for an ultrasound to check for blockages in my intestinal tract. I go through test after test, and yet there are no answers. To make matters worse, I am beginning to have no feelings for my daughters—*nothing*. This unimaginable emptiness is horrifying, and the guilt I feel is unbearable.

Now I am too weak to do anything but lie in my bed. My mum and dad are becoming increasingly worried by the updates from Neil and decide to fly from Australia to help. I can see the fear and concern in their eyes as they take in my frailty and weakness. At one point, my dad sits on my bed, holding my hand, and for the first time since my grandma—his mum—died, I see tears in his eyes.

"We can't lose you. You keep us all together. Hold on. You can't leave us," he says with deep pain and worry in his voice.

My heart is breaking. I am causing so much pain for so many people I love dearly. Why won't this just stop?

The physical drain finally peaks when I collapse in the hallway on the way back from the bathroom, unable to support my own weight. My mum rushes to my side and begs desperately, "I think your doctor is missing the boat, honey. Please get a second opinion. You are wasting away to nothing."

I feel numb—a failure, weak, pathetic, useless, and no good to anyone. I ask myself, "How is it possible that I can look at my girls or at Neil and have no emotions, no feelings for them, nothing? What is wrong with me? Can someone *please* help?"

Mum and Dad return to Australia a couple of weeks later, and I am having mixed feelings about their departure. Sad that they are leaving, I am also relieved that I will not have to see in their eyes the pain I am causing them.

It is Friday, October 22, 2004, and I know I cannot keep going; it has to end. The darkness is unbearable, the sadness and desperation are all-encompassing. This is my first real thought of suicide, and I am filled with relief that I can choose to end this, though I am consumed with fear. I begin to put a plan in motion: I make my way slowly to the pantry, and I grab every pill bottle I can hold. I retreat to the safety of my bedroom and, crying hysterically, I begin to open the bottles.

No, you can't do this, I think, *what about the girls? What about Neil? If you do this, it will destroy them. Well, I'm already doing a good job of that right now. Wouldn't they be better off without me?* I argue with myself, the inner turmoil unendurable. Suddenly, my best friend, Sandra, fills my thoughts. One year ago, her sister ended her life by suicide, and I have seen firsthand the pain it has caused. *Do I really want to cause her that kind of pain again?* I wonder.

For a brief moment, my thoughts are rational: *What am I doing? I can't do this!* In a frenzy of anger, resentment, and hatred toward myself, I gather up all the bottles, return them to the pantry, and find the Yellow Pages. I stumble back to my bedroom, collapse on the bed, weak and exhausted, without any hope. I pick up the phone, open the phone book to the front page, and call the 24-Hour Crisis Line provided by Distress Centre.[1] As a woman answers, I feel an uneasy knot in my stomach, but soon her calm, soothing voice reassures me. She is caring and helpful, listening attentively, not judging me, and all the while asking questions gently. For the first time, I feel that someone really understands and cares.

---

[1] Distress Centre, visit www.distresscentre.com
For worldwide listings of 24-hour crisis lines, visit www.iasp.info.

Among the questions she asks me is, "Have you had any suicidal thoughts? Do you have a plan?"

Ashamed of myself, I lie by omission. "Yes, I have had suicidal thoughts. I feel like everything is hopeless and the only way for it to stop is for me not to be alive," I tell her, leaving out any mention of my plan and of my gathering the pills.

She asks me to give her Neil's work number, and one of her colleagues phones him. She remains on the phone with me, keeping me calm until Neil arrives home. Then she speaks with him briefly, instructing him to take me to the South Calgary Medical Centre where there is a mental health unit.

We go to the clinic, and after a long wait, we are taken into a private room where we are met by a counselor and a doctor. Both agree that I need to see the psychiatrist as soon as possible, and they schedule an appointment for me for Monday. They send us home with strict instructions for Neil to keep a watchful eye on me.

We are both now realizing just how serious this is. I refrain from telling Neil about how close I came to taking my life. Neil is watching carefully, ensuring that I rest while he takes care of the girls and keeps them quiet. The three nights are long, and it seems like forever until Monday. I am terrified of what the psychiatrist will say and what he will do.

Entering a Foreign World

On Monday, October 24, 2004, we meet with a psychiatrist. Within ten minutes, he determines that I must be admitted to the psychiatric ward. He instructs Neil to take me to Emergency at the hospital where we can wait until a bed becomes available. When we arrive at Emergency, we are ushered into a private room, which to my horror, looks just like a room in the movies: a cold, white cell with minimal furniture and with cameras. Instantly I feel ill, and my breathing becomes horribly labored.

"Oh, my God, what has happened to me, Neil?" I ask him desperately.

Neil tries continually to lighten my spirits by making jokes, but nothing works. I am petrified of the unknown, and I am wondering what is going to happen to me. We wait and wait and wait for what seems an eternity. After some time, Neil tells me he must go back to work. Now here I am in this cold place, left alone with the door locked from the outside, a frightened little girl in a woman's body. *It must be a nightmare,* I say to myself. *What am I doing here? I don't need to be here. Please, Neil, come and get me and take me home. I have to get out of here!*

At last, I am led to the psychiatric ward where I am placed on twenty-four-hour supervision, which means that I may not leave the ward. I feel as though I am entering a foreign world, and I am overwhelmed with fear and anxiety. I am taken to my room, and I collapse on the bed in a heap and sob helplessly. Eventually I get up and walk aimlessly up and down the corridor, pacing, crying, and not knowing what to do, where to go, or who to talk to. I feel trapped and alone, and my mind keeps telling me, *I shouldn't be here. I don't belong here. I need to get out of here!* I fall to the ground at the nurses' station, still crying uncontrollably, terrified of not knowing what lies ahead for me.

Patients crying on the floor must be a regular occurrence because no one is coming to my aid or even paying attention to me; patients and staff just walk past me as though I am a piece of furniture. I turn to the only friends I seem to have—my cigarettes—and spend most of the day in the secure outdoor smoking area attached to the ward. I light smoke after smoke, and withdraw and hide completely.

On my second day in the ward, I meet with my designated psychiatrist. Immediately I judge this woman as being cold, uncaring, matter-of-fact, and lacking compassion. I decide she has absolutely no idea what it is I am experiencing or feeling, and I fight her help with everything in me. It seems to me that every question she asks me is rehearsed, as though she is simply going through the motions. I think to myself, *What does she really care how I think and feel? She can't possibly understand.*

Nighttime is unbearably slow in coming, and as it does, I begin to panic because I know what lies ahead. Ward curfew and lights-out is set for 10:00 p.m., but for me, sleep is something in the past. When the night nurse comes in each hour to check on the patients, flashlight shining on each person in turn, I thrust up my hand in sarcasm, anger, and frustration. I spend hour after hour without sleep. I am averaging two hours of interrupted sleep; nothing is helping.

Finally, after two long, drawn-out, miserable nights, they add another drug to the cocktail that they hope will help me sleep. Mercifully it works, and sleep comes at last.

I am having an awful pain in my ribs, and slowly it is getting worse and becoming unbearable. Now I am not sleeping again because it is impossible to get comfortable; the pain prods me awake—as if I need another enemy in the battle for sleep. I am experiencing increasing shortness of breath and pain each time I breathe in. The pain is incredible, and I am yelling at the nurses to get me an X-ray, but they refuse.

I am finally sent for an X-ray, I think, in part, because I am complaining constantly of pain. Nothing abnormal shows on the X-ray: ribs, shoulders, and chest are all fine. I demand to see a chiropractor, insisting pigheadedly that regardless of what the X-rays show, there is something wrong. Once again, my request is refused.

Fortunately, my sister-in-law, Debbie, takes me to a chiropractor since clearly I cannot drive myself and I have never been to one before. As I fill out the forms, I find myself overcome by deep fear from the warnings that say, "We are not responsible for possible injuries that may result." Debbie sees the fear in my eyes but reassures me. She puts her arms around me and tells me I need not go in if I don't want to see the chiropractor, but I decide to go. The chiropractor is extraordinarily gentle and kind. He tells me that at least four of my ribs are out of alignment. He works around my skin and bones to do all that he can to help me. He gives me some relief from the awful pain.

Over the next couple of days, my closest friends come to visit with me, and yet I continue to deny that I need to be here. Tina brings with her a pile of magazines. As we sit on a bench outside, I continue to wear the mask that says, "Everything is okay." Though I am hospitalized in a psychiatric ward, I continue to be dishonest, not only with the friends who come to see me, but most significantly, with myself. I know they can see I am not well, though no words need to be spoken: my extreme weight loss, the dullness of my skin, and the emptiness in my eyes give it away. My friends see it clearly, and yet I continue to deny that anything is wrong.

Sandra visits on her days off. I am heartbroken when I see the pain in her eyes. She lost her sister to suicide only a year ago, and I feel guilty that I am causing her to relive her loss and her pain. Shawn and Tanis come by for a visit. It is obvious that Tanis, who studied psychology, can see through me. In a quiet, dark corner, she and I share one of the deepest conversations I have had since I've been here, and yet, I still deny that anything is wrong.

Gradually, I befriend some of the other patients on the ward. As I learn more about each of them, I am shocked at their stories. One woman witnessed the suicide of her seventeen-year-old son when he put a shotgun in his mouth. For almost six years, she has been in and out of the ward as a result of the deep depression she has experienced because of her grief and guilt. A woman suffering from manic depression (now called bipolar disorder) tells me of the horrors of this nightmarish mental illness. She has lost count of the number of times she has been to this ward. In the hallway, in the same spot, day after day, a woman rolls her cigarettes, keeping to herself except for the occasional raising of her head that shows a blank and empty expression on her face. A young man diagnosed as schizophrenic paces the hallway swearing and banging the walls. Two hours later, he sits in the same hallway and, with incredible talent, plays his guitar and sings soft, beautiful, blues music.

There is one woman on the ward who frightens me. The word is that she does not have a name and she was found wandering the streets. She stays in the twenty-four-hour observation room, which we refer to as the fishbowl. It is opposite the nurses' station and has floor-to-ceiling windows. I walk by the fishbowl, stop, and look in, and our eyes meet. I am overcome by absolute fear, and yet, I cannot stop staring. Her eyes are filled with anger—nothing else, only anger. I am so petrified by this exchange that I do not look at her again. Every time I see her coming toward me, I take a detour in another direction or walk with my head down.

I respond to one particular patient in disbelief and in thorough sadness that fills my heart. A well-groomed and good-looking man, I think in his midthirties, wanders the ward in a hospital gown and nothing else. One day, we are sitting next to each other in the common room. I am taken with his demeanor and his handsome looks and am curious, so I strike up a conversation with him.

"How long have you been here?" I ask in innocence and without expecting the answer he gives me.

"I've been here for three months. I have never been allowed to leave the ward because I am on twenty-four-hour suicide watch. They just don't get it! I want to die, and no one can stop me, so I wish they would just let me do it." He sounds rational and clear. I am speechless. I have no idea how to respond to him.

Even though I still feel that I don't belong on the ward, I am beginning to settle into the routine. I am grateful for the prepared meals and for not having to perform the daily activities that had proven too difficult for me. Finally, I am eating and keeping down my food, and I am beginning to rest more. I decide I would like to have a morning bath. The bathroom that has a bathtub is located near the nurses' station.

Often I have wondered why it was so close by, and now I know. As I undress, I feel dizzy and faint; something is wrong. I press the call button, and by the time the nurse arrives, my vision is gone completely. I collapse in a cold sweat on the chair. My pulse has gone dangerously low. When I wake, I am lying on my bed with machines hooked up to me and with numerous doctors and nurses standing around me. Later, my doctor explains to me that sometimes when medication is changed, a patient can get worse before getting better. The new antipsychotic medication they gave me made me definitely worse, and they take me off it immediately.

The days are monotonous. It seems as though I have been here forever, and yet I have been here for less than a week. I leave the ward as often as possible to walk the grounds and to smoke like crazy, sucking in ferociously what I see as my only rebellion and my only taste of freedom in the cool, October weather.

The "old" Lee was so creative, organized, and focused. She had the ability to create something with little effort, to do crosswords and other puzzles with ease, to develop single-handedly a plan to reroute numerous aircraft and crew, to manage staff, multitask, organize, and plan anything. Yet now, performing the simplest of tasks, such as a word search puzzle, is next to impossible. After trying to find the third word, I give up in frustration, anger, and sadness.

I decide to give painting a try. I sit in the dining room with paint supplies and a desire to paint a picture. It is painstakingly slow for me to paint a simple picture of a lily to give to my girls. Because of weakness, fatigue, and the medication cocktail I am taking, my hands shake constantly. I must hold my right hand steady with my left so that I can keep the paintbrush still. What normally would have taken me an hour to finish took me almost eight hours.

For some reason, this painting is a huge awakening, a definite shift. I have a realization that I *am* sick; I know I need help and I must let in the people who want to help me. Now, instead of pretending I am okay, I am beginning to allow people to see my pain, to see the depths of my darkness, and to see how the simplest of tasks have become so difficult.

For the first time since I've been here, Neil brings our older daughter to visit with me. It is just before Halloween. I have not seen her for a week, and I have no feelings of longing or of missing her and her sister. I wonder what kind of mother I am. She is dressed in her angel Halloween costume. For the first time in a very long time, I feel a touch of joy. As she walks down the hallway toward me, the same hallway where the woman rolls her cigarettes and where the young man paces back and forth, the length of the hallway is lightened with her radiance and innocence. A different light illuminates the hallway that I, too, pace.

In my room, she cuddles up with me on the bed. I can feel her discomfort, confusion, and fear. I wonder, *What is going on in her mind?*

"Mommy, when are you coming home? I miss you!" she says, pain showing in her beautiful blue eyes.

"Sweetie, I don't know—when the doctors say Mommy is better," I answer her honestly, knowing full well there is no way I can go home right now. I simply would not be able to handle it.

I give her the painting of the lily that I had created with such care. I feel warmth in my heart, a connection and a little pride. I don't think she understands fully the meaning behind the painting, but something tells me she does have some sense of it.

I hold Neil and give him a kiss of thanks. He is taken aback by my display of affection, something he hasn't seen for a very long time. Then he tells me he is going to take the girls to Winnipeg for Halloween to visit his brother and sister-in-law. Instantly, all the positive emotion I am feeling is replaced by fear. *Oh, my God, he is leaving me,* I think. *I am absolutely alone. He can't handle it anymore.*

Any and every story a sick mind can invent is teeming in my mind. Still, I don't want Neil to know my fears. I want him to have some normality in his life, to see some sanity in all this, so I remain quiet and mask my fear. After they leave, I am filled with guilt, and once again I feel hopeless. *I am ruining them. I am causing them so much pain. They are so much better off without me,* I tell myself.

The patients in the psychiatric ward call the weekends the "graveyard," and soon I understand why. Minimal staff and many patients out on weekend passes make the ward a quiet and eerie place. This is my first weekend, and knowing that Neil is away I feel lost, lonely, and afraid. It is Saturday, October 30. I have been given a day pass, and my mother-in-law comes to pick me up. I feel her underlying energy of judgment, and so I ask her if she would like one of the nurses to explain what I am experiencing. We all sit together in the dining room, and the nurse explains the impact and the effects of major depression and anxiety. I, too, am educated by this meeting. With tremendous patience, the nurse answers all of my mother-in-law's questions. With a little more understanding on her part, my mother-in-law takes me to her home where it is just her and me.

I am longing to have a bath in privacy and to shave my legs. We are not allowed razors in the psychiatric ward. With little energy, I note that I have come to such a place of defeat that when my mother-in-law comes into the bathroom repeatedly to check on me while I am bathing, I offer no resistance, I say nothing. Here I am, absolutely vulnerable, naked and weak, and yet I feel the need to apologize for the state of my body, bones kept in place by flesh.

She orders Chinese food and leaves me while she goes to pick it up. For the first time in what seems like forever, I am left alone. My thoughts go continually to the kitchen drawer where the knives are kept. "What the hell is going on?" I ask myself. I picture myself cutting my wrist. The anxiety is overwhelming, and I am overcome with fear and panic. *Please let her come home soon, please, please ...* Finally she arrives, but I continue to be overwhelmed by anxiety. Once again I don my mask, believing she has no idea of the inner pain and turmoil I am suffering. After I finished the meal, to my relief, she drives me back to the hospital.

I Want the Pain to End

If you're going through hell, keep going.

—Winston Churchill

I have heard nothing from Neil. My mind is racing. I am lost in loneliness, feeling profoundly abandoned. I think, *Why would he want to stick it out with me anyway? They must be having a great time without the stress of having to worry about me! They are so much better off without me!*

It is Halloween, Sunday, October 31. From the moment I wake, I am consumed with a deep desire to end my existence. I lie in my bed and write a note to my family. Then I walk into the bathroom and look at myself in the mirror. The person looking back at me is skin and bones: her collarbone protrudes; she looks gaunt and has a deep sadness and hopelessness in her eyes. I cannot continue like this. I am causing everyone so much pain. I can no longer deal with this horror.

Then, in the mirror's reflection, I notice the shower curtain ... will it do the trick? I turn to the shower and take the curtain in my hands, twisting it so that it is tight. I pull on it a couple of times to ensure the rings will hold. I wrap the curtain tightly around my neck. I pull it tighter and tighter and then I begin to bend my knees so that the curtain will tighten even more around my neck. I am becoming light-headed, and I am having difficulty breathing. I let the rod hold more of my weight. One of the rings snaps. I can't do it! I crumple to the ground in utter defeat, even more depressed and sobbing uncontrollably. "I don't even have the strength to kill myself ... I am so pathetic!"

To my Dear Family & Friends

Nothing I can write will explain to you why? The pain won't go away & i'm not strong enough to go on.

Please live your lives to the fullest & enjoy every minute & know I will always be here with you.

Neil you are so full of love & life, I am so sorry to do this to you, but please try & move on. Neil you are a wonderful husband & father always know that. I love you & I'm so sorry.

I have asked God for help & forgiveness & to open is arms to all of you.

All my Love
Lee
X O X O X

Mum & Dad You guys are wonderful you have done a great job I Love You

My actual suicide note; I have erased my
daughters' names circa October 31, 2004.

32

After breakfast, I continue to be consumed by thoughts of death—ending it all and stopping the pain. I make my way to the top floor of the parking lot. A vehicle is backing up, so I pretend that I am looking at the view of the reservoir while I wait for them to leave. All clear, I climb up on top of the pillar. I stand here, pausing for a moment to look around and at the surface below. Briefly I think back to ten years before, when my ex-boyfriend leapt to his death from a fourteen-story building. If he could do it, so can I. I stand there, looking down at the concrete below. "This isn't high enough. What if I survive? Then I will be mentally screwed up *and* physically battered and broken," I say out loud, though no one is there to hear me.

For what seems forever, I continue to stand there, completely alone. The conflict raging inside me is devastating: yes, no, yes, no, yes, *no* ... I can't do this. I step down and lie on the concrete, once again feeling thoroughly defeated.

"I am pathetic, a waste of fucking skin, a waste of existence," I yell out and continue to lie on the concrete, a blubbering mess. Eventually, I go back to the ward and lie on my bed, sobbing. Totally alone, desperate and hopeless, all I want to do is die, but I can't do it.

"You are *so* pathetic!" I say out loud, but no one is around, no one hears me; it's just me, all by myself.

I am brutally aware of my frailty, how desperate I have become, and the delicate thread between life and death. Also, I am far too aware of the lack of observation on the part of staff on this spooky "graveyard" day. I disappear for hours on end around the hospital grounds, in spite of the fact I am supposed to be gone for only one hour at a time. Yet no one seems to notice my lengthy absences. No one is aware, because I choose to be alone. I choose not to speak with a nurse, and I choose to be consumed by ending my life. Quite frankly, I have no idea why. All I know is that I want to die.

My God, it strikes me it's only lunchtime. This morning does not want to end. As the minutes tick by, each one is filled with emptiness and desperation, loneliness and sadness, and despair and grief. I make an appearance at lunch, and then once again disappear quickly onto the hospital grounds. This time, though, I am on a mission—a mission to find something sharp. I wander way off the grounds and stumble across a pile of broken beer bottles. I search through them and find the sharpest shards, picking several, just in case.

It is gray and cold. The sky is filled with dark, stormy clouds. Lifeless trees surround me as I sit by the reservoir, shards of glass in hand. Time crawls, feeling like forever, as I sit numb, empty, and entirely alone.

"Well, this is it. It's time," I say out loud, holding glass in my right hand. "God, I am sorry. I just can't keep going on. If you love me, you will help me right now," I say, looking into the sky.

I try to break skin. The glass is not sharp enough! Once again, I begin to cry. Then something sweeps over me. "You fucking idiot! Just press harder! How difficult can it be?" The frustration and anger I feel for myself are building. I apply greater pressure and draw blood. As I see the blood, I am surprised that I feel nothing, no pain. I am numb. *This will be easy,* I think to myself.

Like a whisper in the wind, I hear something above me. Startled, I look up to see two female sparrows perched on a branch right above me. I stop cutting and lie back on the cold, rocky ground. I lie there just looking at them, and it seems as though these two little birds are looking right back at me with inquisitiveness. A flutter in my heart makes me stop and listen. Suddenly, I feel a glimmer of hope, light, and love. And then, in the faces of these sweet birds, I see the faces of my two beautiful daughters smiling down on me with unconditional love.

In this breathtaking moment, the anger and frustration that were just present have been replaced by something entirely different. Now tears are flowing freely, and yet they are a different type of tears. I feel warmth within my heart, warmth that feels foreign and still, somehow familiar.

"Are you here to answer my prayers?" I ask the sparrows. As I lie here, I understand the message. These sparrows, representing my daughters, are my angels. I choose to believe that I have been given a gift. I decide here and now that I want to live.

What I Know Now That I Didn't Know Then

- What I do for work does not define who I am.
- Anger is not an unhealthy emotion. I need to talk about it and respond in a healthy way.
- Wearing a mask suppresses and prolongs pain.
- I need to be accepting of others' fears and recognize it is not personal or about me.
- I need to be honest when someone discards my feelings.
- When in doubt, seek a second opinion.
- I need to take responsibility and advocate for my own health.
- There is no shame in asking for help.
- I need to be open and willing to receiving help.
- Help is readily available when I ask.
- Children are resilient, understanding, and pure love.
- I am not alone.
- Awareness is a step to emotional freedom.
- Life is precious, and there is always hope.

Chapter 3

Acceptance: Surrendering and Letting Go

We must accept life for what it actually is—a challenge to our quality without which we should never know of what stuff we are made or grown to our full stature.

—Ida R. Wylie

As I lie under the tree with the two sparrows still watching me, I am not feeling quite so alone. I let go, release, and surrender. "God, I don't know what to do. I don't know how I am going to do it. I know I am very sick and that I need your help to live."

I lie here crying, releasing and accepting just how sick I am. I feel as though a huge burden has been lifted from me, and I am feeling almost serene and peaceful. I have absolutely no idea what is happening right now, but I am not going to move. It seems that hours have passed, but I do not leave this place of calm until the crisp, cold air sinks into my skin and bones.

"What just happened? What do I do now?" I wonder and realize that I haven't a clue. What I *do* know is that I must accept it and allow it to unfold. It turns out that nearly four hours have passed since I left the ward, and yet no one questions me or asks where I have been. *No one cares. I could have been dead down by the water, and no one would have blinked an eye,* I think to myself.

A quiet strong voice speaks gently, *Lee, of course they care. You didn't tell anyone where you were going.*

It is Monday, November 1, 2004, one day after I longed to end my life, and Neil arrives for our family meeting with my psychiatrist. I almost expected never to see him again. I just hold him, feeling deep joy, love, and relief that he hasn't actually left me. I talk a lot and cry a lot. Neil asks many questions, his concern and confusion unmistakable. Still, I tell neither of them what had happened to me the day before, how deep and dark I had gone, nor about the glimmer of light that saved me. I decide once again to stay quiet and to keep it to myself; as it is, people think I'm crazy. If I tell them what happened, I will never get out of here. Somewhere in my soul, a shift has occurred; I have hope, and I feel the relief that acceptance brings.

Leslie comes to visit me, and she is the first person I tell about my day, though I do not let her know the full extent of my desperate acts. I pull down my turtleneck and show her the marks left by the shower curtain.

Anxiety and depression continue to have a hold on me. I continue to have suicidal thoughts, although now I am supported by a strong, calm, and quiet voice within that helps me to prevail. *Lee, just get through this next minute. That's all you need to do right now. Get through this next minute. You can do that!*

Tina arrives for a visit, and we decide to go to Chinook Mall and walk around. Finally I let her in a little, giving her bits and pieces of the darkness in which I've been living, although I refrain from telling her about Sunday. I have a few anxiety attacks as we walk around, but I am able to manage them quietly. It is plain for me to see how much Tina wants to understand my depression; she asks thoughtful questions, and I feel that she understands at least a little.

I finally open up to some of the nurses—in particular, Judy. Initially, I am fearful of her, intimidated by her strength and confidence. Yet, in a curious way, I feel drawn to her. On a few occasions, I spend the evening with her in one of the boardrooms. She guides me through visioning exercises to calm my mind and relax me. Her voice is soothing. Being in her presence begins to give me the sense that someone truly wishes to help me and actually cares about me and my illness. I look forward to our meetings now, and when she is not on duty, I feel lost and abandoned.

It is Tuesday, November 2, and Neil brings our one-year-old for a visit. It is so wonderful to see her that my cheeks are burning from smiling. She has grown so much and is so beautiful. I feel no anxiety as I embrace this wonderful moment of feeding her a bottle and hearing her giggle. At one point, not so long ago, I blamed her for my anxiety. Now I know how wrong I was. Experiencing this deep joy is a gift, and it gives me a powerful willingness to keep going.

I begin to participate in some of the many workshops the hospital facilitates: cooking, cognitive behavioral therapy, exercise, and recreational activities that include walks along the reservoir. At the spot where I almost took my life, I pause for a moment. I am grateful to be within a group, to feel the presence of everyone else, and to feel the need to continue walking. It allows me to reflect quietly and quickly, and I find that my reflection is one of gratitude for the two little sparrows and for the choice I made to live.

Finding Lee

Over the next couple of days, I find I am feeling a little more like myself. I have been using the tools I've been taught to calm my anxiety. By keeping myself active, I find I have more energy, and I am able to smile and think positively. I go to the gym today and play basketball and then go to the occupational therapy kitchen to bake cookies. We are taught the steps to make simple sugar cookies as though we are children baking for the first time. In some cases, this is true. One woman needs full direction and constant help from our instructor. A young man continually asks questions about each step. In this moment, I realize just how serious and debilitating mental illness is.

On November 6 and 7, 2004, I am given a weekend pass: two days and one night at home to see how I will do there. On this cold Saturday morning, Neil comes to pick me up. The girls are with his parents so that I may ease myself into being at home again. I am learning how to be more open with Neil and how to let him know what I am truly feeling. Still, the old patterns emerge. I want to protect him; I don't want him to stress and worry more than he already does. So I give him only glimpses of the anxiety and worry I am feeling.

As we walk into the house, I am overcome with every emotion imaginable: love, fear, joy, sadness, eagerness, frustration, gratitude, resentment—the list goes on and on. I do have an underlying feeling of relief in knowing that if I become too overwhelmed, I may go right back to the hospital.

The quiet strong voice continues to reassure me and to give me strength: *Lee, you can do this. You will do this. Give it time and take baby steps.*

In the afternoon, Neil's mom and dad bring the girls home. At first I am overjoyed to be with them, to feel their innocence, purity, and unconditional love. Soon though, motherly instincts kick in, and I want to do everything with them and to be everything to them. I feel utterly helpless that I am unable to fulfill that for them. Guilt and shame begin to creep in again, making me feel anxious. But now I have some tools with which to cope.

Lee, breathe. Close your eyes and quiet your mind; this too shall pass, the quiet strong voice tells me reassuringly. And pass it does, as time and time again I take myself through this process: baby steps, baby steps, baby steps.

On Sunday, I am grateful to go back to the safety of the psychiatric ward where my meals are made for me and where I have no responsibility for others. I reflect on my visit home with almost constant fear and anxiety; I know I am not ready to go back yet. I can't do this.

Lee, you will when you are ready, says the quiet strong voice.

For the next two nights, I do not sleep. I am kept awake by the constant chatter in my mind, a pounding headache, fear, worry about the possibility I will be discharged, and a weird, tense feeling in my jaw. When I meet with my psychiatrist, I tell her that I am not sleeping well because my mind is racing. I have had a pounding headache for two days, and my jaw feels like it is locked. She tells me that she sees me as a results-driven person and that when I don't achieve what I want, the anxiety and depression are triggered. She believes this is the cause of the headaches and of the tension in my jaw. She encourages me to change my thought process so that I do not put so much pressure on myself. "Easier said than done, lady," I say to myself.

The hospital recreation program sets up a rock-climbing outing. In spite of having a great deal of fear, I agree to go, though the reasons not to go are plentiful. I've never done this before. I am weak physically, so how on earth am I going to be able to climb? What if I fall and break every bone in my body? What if I drop the person I am supposed to support? Soon though, I discover I am not alone in my thoughts and fears. The other patients who have come along feel just as I do. As we talk about it, each of us realizes we are not alone.

To my utter surprise, I not only participate, I actually climb all the way to the top of the wall. Even though I am skin and bone and very frail both physically and mentally, I find the strength to overcome my fears and climb that wall. As I sit in the halter at the top of the wall, I look down with an enfolding feeling of pride and relief.

Lee, you are much stronger than you think, the quiet strong voice tells me lovingly.

This proves to be another turning point for me, giving me insight into the inner strength that arms me, even though I have been blind to it.

Going Home

> Courage doesn't always roar. Sometimes courage is the little voice at the end of the day that says I'll try again tomorrow.
>
> —Mary Anne Radmacher

Each day, the baby steps that carry me through, moment by moment, are getting longer. Right now, I focus on moving through one hour at a time. Now that I have surrendered and accepted help from the staff, I have begun to participate in life once more and I am feeling stronger each day. However, the tension in my jaw and the continual headaches worry me. Physically, I still feel weak, but that is okay.

My psychiatrist is impressed with the progress I am making. Now I am absolutely honest in every little detail, every single emotion, every fear, and about my physical pain. After listening to me right to the end of my revelations, she says to me, "Well, Lee, I believe you are almost ready to be released."

What? *Did you not hear me? I am still filled with fear. I'm not ready to leave!* I am screaming all this silently, unable to speak it out loud to her.

She tells me that the medication cocktail I am taking right now will form the foundation and the balance I need and that I will more than likely be discharged next week. Shortly after my discharge, I will begin the four-week outpatient day program. If it's required, she will continue to see me after I am discharged. Nothing she says reassures me in any way.

My emotions are all over the place: this is good, I can finally get out of here ... oh my God, what am I going to

43

do? ... it's going to be okay; help will be available ... who is going to take care of me?; how am I going to take care of myself and my family? Fear takes over and smothers any joy I might feel about being "let out."

Yet the quiet strong voice tells me, *Lee, take baby steps and you will be okay.* In this moment, I feel a scintilla of hope.

My emotions continue to be a roller coaster, although they are not quite as wild as they have been. I continue to listen to the quiet strong voice, and I continue to share my thoughts and feelings with the nurses and my psychiatrist. In particular, Judy, my favorite nurse, provides me with visioning tools, meditations, and ways to calm my mind. She always takes the time to help me prepare for the reality of going home, using a straightforward honesty that both frightens and reassures me.

It is November 15, 2004, and I am released from the hospital. Not knowing what lies ahead and feeling overwhelming fear, I pack my belongings and prepare to leave the room I have called home for the past three weeks. It feels so much longer than three weeks; this place that at first I resisted has become a sanctuary for me. I have made some friends, and as I leave, I am struck suddenly by grief.

As patients, we are discouraged from exchanging contact information, so I find the good-byes tough, knowing that I may never see any of them again. As we embrace, I see that the woman who lost her son to suicide seven years before has a tear in her eye. The woman with manic depression, who has been in and out of the hospital, hugs me and whispers words of encouragement in my ear. A young girl, whom I have befriended recently, gives me a warm hug, and I can feel every ounce of her fear and sadness. Saying good-bye to her especially saddens me. I have been present for her several times in the past week both before and after her electroconvulsive therapy treatments (at the time, I only knew of this as shock treatment). This nineteen-year-old girl is lost, alone, and abandoned by her family; as a mother, my heart breaks for her. Silently I say a prayer for her, embrace her, and fight to let go. The woman who stays in the room next to mine, and with whom I have had many deep and insightful conversations, gives me a teddy bear and thanks me for our friendship.

And so it is afternoon, and I am officially released from the psychiatric ward. Neil arrives after work to take me home. As I leave the ward, armed with all my medications and my belongings, I look back and suddenly am overcome by fear and doubt; I am petrified. My head begins to pound even worse than before, and the tension in my jaw is nearly unbearable. As we drive home, I share some of my fear with Neil, who reassures me that I am not expected to do anything and that I will not be left alone with the girls until I am ready.

My first evening at home is uneventful. We sit downstairs as a family and watch a movie. The girls don't want me out of their sight. They cuddle peacefully with me, and I wonder how they can know to be silent and still. Yet, they do know. After the movie, Neil puts them to bed, and I get myself ready for bed. As I take my sleeping pill, I pray that I will have a solid and restful sleep. I lay in bed, feeling grateful for the comfort and space of our king-size bed, the beautiful sheets, and the weight of the bedding on top of me. Even though I adorned my hospital bed with some personal blankets and my own pillow, it never felt comfortable. Sleep comes easily to me.

I wake in the morning feeling lost for a moment and then realize I'm home. I feel a little smile cross my face, and then I feel fearful. I ask myself, "What am I going to do? How am I going to get through this day without the routine of the hospital?" Thankfully, Neil is quick to notice my anxiety. He holds me and reassures me that everything is okay.

The quiet strong voice pops up: *Lee, you are loved.*

It has been quite a while since I have heard the constant chatter of the girls. It doesn't stop. I think, *Stop talking, just stop!* My head is pounding. For a brief moment, I lose it, and the girls' faces fill with disbelief and fear. Thankfully, Neil steps in.

"Girls, Mommy needs some quiet. Do you understand? She is still not well," he tells them lovingly yet with authority.

The girls heed him and for a little while play silently, which gives me the opportunity to embrace and to cope with the panic attack and pounding headache I am having.

Lee, breathe; close your eyes and quiet your mind; this too shall pass, says the quiet strong voice reassuringly.

I survive another attack. With each one, I feel more confident that I am able to deal with them, accepting them and not fighting them. Nurse Judy gave me sound advice and a valuable tool: *Do not* resist or fight your anxiety; embrace it. Ask yourself what is triggering it and say your mantra: "Lee, breathe; close your eyes and quiet your mind; this too shall pass."

What I Know Now That I Didn't Know Then

- When I surrender and let go, I am open to help and support.
- With acceptance comes a sense of release and freedom.
- I need to listen to the quiet strong voice of reason and resilience.
- Relationships deepen when I am open and honest.
- I need to be open to learning new tools and lessons.
- Participating in life is a gift, no matter how big or small.
- Gratitude is a way of being.
- I need to apply the tools and lessons I learn.
- Never assume; it is not up to me to make a decision for another person.
- This too shall pass; it always does.
- I am much stronger than I think.
- Bravery is also in the small acts of courage.

Chapter 4

Action: Taking Baby Steps

The self is not something ready-made, but something
in continuous formation through choice of action.

—John Dewey

It is Wednesday, November 17, 2004. I reflect on how far I have come, and yet I know I still have a long way to go. Yesterday I had a massage, which helped the headache a little, but still I have a great deal of tension in my jaw and shoulders. It is so good to be home. My older daughter is so happy to have me back, though I sense she is quite tentative. My younger daughter interacts with me much more; I feel her need and desire to connect and play with me. At times, I feel tremendously guilty to think I have missed out on so much. Emotionally, I am doing pretty well. I need to remind myself constantly that it is going to take time and that I need to be patient.

At dinner this evening, my older daughter "has attitude." She refuses to eat her supper, and Neil is frustrated and furious. My chest is burning, my breathing becomes rapid, and I can sense a panic attack coming.

My head is throbbing, and my jaw is clenched tight. I can't move.

Lee, breathe; close your eyes and quiet your mind; this too shall pass, says the quiet strong voice gently ... And pass it does.

I take each day as it comes, with baby steps. I continue to use the tools I was taught while in hospital. Even though I still have feelings of fear and doubt, the despair and hopelessness are not as prevalent. I still use several tools to help me cope with the anxiety attacks and with quieting my mind: meditation, visualization, recognizing and accepting *all* emotions, being in the moment (no forward thinking), and breathing.

As I begin to feel stronger, Neil must remind me constantly to take it easy. For the past two days, everything I have seen that needs to be done, I have done. I have even been doing things that don't need doing. I clean the closets. I change lightbulbs. I clean the house. And I even begin to do the Christmas shopping.

"Am I trying to hide in busyness again?" I ask myself. I remember the conversation with my psychiatrist about being results driven. I give myself permission to let go of the need to do everything, and I read again something I had written: "Lower my standards on things that aren't top priority and accept imperfection."

It is Tuesday, November 30, 2004, and I awake bright and early. Well, not exactly bright, since it is 6:00 a.m. and dark outside. It has been a long time since I have needed to be up at this hour. My body fights the early rising, my head aching and jaw clenching unbearably in tension. I wonder if these physical ailments could really be symptoms of anxiety. My psychiatrist insists they are, and it is interesting to note that they are more intense when I am feeling fearful. The fear today stems from the fact that I am returning to the same hospital where I spent three of the darkest and most painful weeks of my life. I question, "How will I react once I am there? How will I feel?" Nervous thoughts and questions fill my mind for the entire drive to the hospital.

As I enter the parking lot, my mind carries me back to the day when, in great physical and mental pain, I climbed the stairs to the top level of this very structure. I can see it. I can feel it. I am disconcerted by the mix of emotions that surface. I sit in the car for a moment, and as I look up, I shake my head in wonder when I see that I have parked my car so that it faces the very window of the room where I spent those three long weeks. While I reflect upon the many emotions I feel, I focus primarily on gratitude. I am grateful that I am still alive, grateful that I have come so far, grateful for life.

The first two days of the outpatient day program are concerned with laying foundations and guidelines. I meet with my therapist, whom I like and connect with instantly. She is a calm woman with a loving and sweet energy. Also, I meet my new psychiatrist, a gentle man; I find it easy to talk to him. We talk about what brought me here, about the changes I've made, and about my plan for moving forward.

Boundaries

It is Thursday, December 2, the third day of the outpatient day program, and construction traffic makes me late. I hate to be late. Normally I would be uptight and stressed about this, but miraculously I find that I am relaxed.

Our first group session is about boundaries. In the first exercise we perform, another participant comes too close to me. I feel the tension building in my neck—it moves into my jaw, and my head begins to pound. The instructions are to "hold your ground" and not move, but instead, to notice how you feel.

The quiet strong voice pops up with, *Lee, breathe; quiet your mind; this too shall pass.*

I soon discover that I make assumptions about what another person's boundaries might be. In the next exercise, I am paired with a woman much shorter than I. Immediately I feel uncomfortable and assume that she must feel that I am looking down on her, so I bend my knees to come to her height. A glazed look sweeps over her eyes, and for a moment I feel frightened.

"What are you doing?" she asks firmly. Though she is tiny in stature, she has a strong and direct personality.

"I think you are uncomfortable because I am so much taller than you, so I'm making myself smaller," I reply.

"You know what. I can't stand it when people do that! It draws more attention to the fact that I'm short. I'm short, okay. That's the way I am, so get over it and don't treat me any differently than you would others!" she says.

Wow. This is a huge wake-up call for me. I consider, "How often do I make assumptions in various aspects of my life, and how often do I make myself feel smaller to make another feel better?"

There's nothing enlightened about shrinking
so that other people won't feel insecure

around you. We are all meant to shine, as children do.

—Marianne Williamson

Our group continues to discuss boundaries, something I have been attempting to create since going home two weeks ago. How easy it is for me to fall into old habits, needing constantly to remind myself that I must create and maintain boundaries for myself. My mental health depends on it.

> Through our conscious creation of boundaries we will develop the ability to establish a sacred container from which to contemplate our oneness. Without this knowledge we will turn desperately to anything that can medicate our dis-ease.
>
> —Rokelle Lerner[1]

I realize quickly how important boundaries are to my life and what an important role they play. It makes perfect sense, and I wonder how I could have been unaware of this concept for so long.

> **Physical Boundaries** *ensure that we can identify where we end and others begin, and can, therefore, protect ourselves against invasion by others.*
>
> —Rokelle Lerner[1]

---

[1] Rokelle Lerner, *Living in the Comfort Zone*, Health Communications, Inc. 1995

In looking back, I see that, other than feeling a panic attack coming when I was performing the exercise with the woman who came too close to me, I don't recall feeling unsafe. I ask myself, "Does this mean that I am comfortable with physical boundaries?" Then I remember the woman in the psychiatric ward who had the anger-filled eyes. I realize I did create a physical boundary with her. I knew I did not want to be near her because I felt unsafe, so without realizing it consciously, I created a physical boundary.

> **Emotional Boundaries** help us to distinguish our own emotions from others', to recognize healthy expressions of our own feelings, and to take full responsibility for our behavior, and not for others.
>
> —Rokelle Lerner[1]

The instructor talks about conversations that are taking place in the common-room areas and that may offend some people. "What conversations? Were they talking about me? Who was offended? What did they do or say?" I am filled instantly with feelings of tightness and burning in my chest, and in my head I make up different stories.

Lee, breathe; these are just stories you are making up, nothing you know for sure to be true; quiet your mind, the quiet strong voice tells me calmly.

Suddenly, I get it! I tend to make up stories in my head when I think someone doesn't like me or when I think I have upset someone. I withdraw and become quiet. I share this realization with the group. To my great surprise, many others can relate to what I say, and immediately

I feel calm. All at once, I feel proud and relieved. By sharing my thoughts openly, others feel free to share theirs, and it is as though a wall comes down. For the first time since this group began, we are engaged in a healthy, open, and honest conversation. We talk about how we are affected *differently* by whether our boundaries are loose, flexible, or rigid. I realize that I have been living my life with boundaries that have been either loose (no door, no roof, just openings) *or* rigid (bars on windows; a fence with barbed wire; and big, heavy doors with deadbolts on them). The types of boundaries I have really wanted all along are flexible ones: a normal house with windows and curtains that open and close.

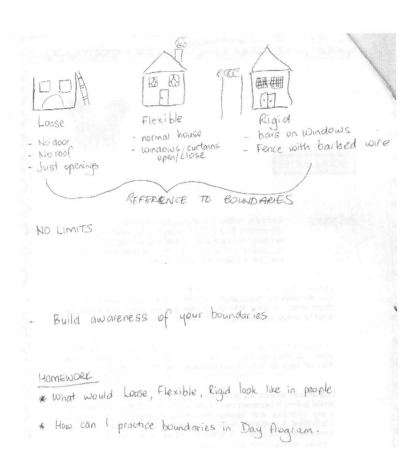

Loose
- No door
- No roof
- Just openings

Flexible
- normal house
- windows/curtains open/close

Rigid
- bars on windows
- Fence with barbed wire

REFERENCE TO BOUNDARIES

NO LIMITS

- Build awareness of your boundaries

HOMEWORK
* What would Loose, Flexible, Rigid look like in people.
* How can I practice boundaries in Day Program.

Notes I took from the session on boundaries
circa December 2, 2004

Intellectual Boundaries allow us to process data from the outside world before it becomes part of our worldview. Rather than waking every morning and letting the world happen to us, healthy intellectual boundaries make us proactive in relationship to our environment and help us to articulate our needs and desires.

—Rokelle Lerner[1]

The word *intellectual* stirs up in me an uneasy feeling, and quickly I am aware of the tapes I play in my head over and over again. I dropped out of school midway through the eleventh grade and did not go to university. The stories I have told myself for a long time are that I am stupid, I am not smart enough, I am dumb, and I am not good enough. Our group talks about how changing the patterns of our perceptions requires us to value our inner wisdom and our intuition. For far too long, I have held these beliefs about myself as true when in fact, they are not. I realize though, I will need to reflect much more because the tapes continue to replay as we work to change our old perceptions.

Spiritual Boundaries allow us to bring the blessings of spirituality into our lives. When we empower ourselves by intentionally choosing our boundaries, we experience dignity, self-respect and we are able to give and receive love in ways that nurture our souls and enhance our serenity.

—Rokelle Lerner[1]

Although I am not a religious person, I have always believed in God. As soon as the instructor says the word *spiritual*, I think, *Oh, no, here we go, now there will be*

---

[1] Rokelle Lerner, *Living in the Comfort Zone.* Health Communications, Inc, 1995

arguments about each person's religious beliefs. I am relieved to discover this is not the case.

"What does *spirituality* mean to you?" we are asked.

I share my fear about what may lie ahead. The instructor assures me that spiritual boundaries consist in honoring the self and becoming in touch with serenity, peace, and calm. I wonder, "Where do I look for this?" I hadn't really thought of spirituality in this way; I realize that I have always been so wrapped up in doing, doing, doing that I never have experienced the simplicity of *being*.

Building a Support Network

> Too often we underestimate the power of a touch, a smile, a kind word, a listening ear, an honest compliment, or the smallest act of caring, all of which have the potential to turn a life around.
>
> —Leo Buscaglia

As we gather to discuss building a support network, I instantly feel uncomfortable. All of my friends are so busy. Besides, I don't know how on earth I can ask them to be part of my support network after having caused them so much worry and pain. I can get through this on my own, without having to worry them any further.

Right at this very moment, we are asked to write down, without thinking about it, what kind of support we need. *Okay, I'm willing to give this a try,* I think quietly to myself, with a somewhat open mind. My hand begins to write: love, emotional support, affirmation, help, time together, being held accountable, information/advice, lighten things up, do things (tasks, babysit), belonging, feeling needed, validate, challenges …

Now we are instructed to write about how we can obtain that support. Again my hand begins to write: community, friends, family, therapist, community center, crisis lines, church, support groups, pets and animals, sports, volunteer, books, the Internet …

We're asked, "What are things I can do in difficult times?" My first thought is: relax and do nothing. Yet, as with the first two exercises, we are instructed to write without thinking. Here I go again: visualize, go for a walk, call a friend, pat the horses, have a hot bath, listen to music, journal, take a deep breath, allow positive thinking …

I am surprised at how easily the words flow. We continue to work through the creation of a support network, identifying key people who could provide support to us in difficult times. For me, difficult times are when I have anxiety attacks, problems with my daughters or family, or when I do not take time for myself.

As we continue our group discussions and as I journal and reflect upon what may get in the way of my using my support network, I become aware of themes emerging: I take on too much; I do not take time for myself; I am not honest and true to myself or others.

"So, how do I move past these barriers and actually ask people for help?" I ask the instructor, sharing with her that throughout this journey, I have done a good job of wearing a mask so that people see me as a happy and healthy person. She gives me many wonderful tips, but one comment in particular really hits home with me.

She looks directly at me and says, "Imagine one of your daughters going through a difficult time. Now imagine she has no one to support her because she chooses not to ask for help."

I stop dead in my tracks, tears welling up in my eyes as I imagine my older daughter alone, in pain, and not asking for help. Immediately I understand how important it is to do this, not only for myself, but also as a model for my daughters. The wall of resistance I have built comes tumbling down. I think about what it would look like if the girls chose to hide behind masks too.

Lee, asking for help is a sign of strength, says the quiet strong voice. *Aha*—I get it.

With this insight filling my heart with a fresh direction, I spend the entire lunch break alone, working diligently on my support network.

WHAT STOPS YOU FROM COMMUNICATING,

- Low Self Esteem
- What other people will think & also fear of how they will react.
- Laziness, illness (Depression)
- Uncertaintity / lack of knowledge of how to be assertive.
- Fear of repercussions (work especially).
- Past experiences - being assertive & knocked back by an aggressive person.
- Fear of Change
- Lack of knowledge about the subject matter

WHAT ASSUMPTIONS OR BELIEFS STOP YOU.

- Equality (power struggle).
- Male / Female
- Cultural
- Up bringing
- Religion

My notes on what would hold me
back circa December 2004.

Embracing Anger

> Where there is anger, there is always pain underneath.
>
> —Eckhart Tolle

It is Monday, December 13, 2004, and I arrive early to my group session. I notice the Christmas tree and the decorations lying in a heap in the common room. After checking with the receptionist, I begin to assemble the tree. As I am doing this, I can feel my chest tightening and my face burns as I gaze at everyone else sitting around, chatting and watching me working by myself. As I begin to decorate the tree, after having assembled it by myself, a woman comes over to help. I become frustrated quickly as I see that she does not put on the lights the way I envision they should go. Then, all of a sudden, my anger turns inward: *You are so pathetic. Here you are getting angry that no one is helping, and then finally someone comes to help and you get frustrated. You are so pathetic!* I feel nauseated by this sudden attack on myself, and I retreat quickly to a corner of the room to write in my journal.

Interestingly, the topic for discussion this morning is anger. I do not realize how much unexpressed anger I hold inside. Mostly the anger is directed toward myself, but also I unleash unhealthy anger upon Neil and my daughters. Learning that anger is a healthy emotion is an eye-opener for me. I have always looked at anger as an emotion to avoid at all costs.

> Our anger may tell us that we are not addressing an important emotional issue in our lives, or that too much of our self—our

beliefs, values, desires, or ambitions—is being compromised in a relationship. Our anger may be a signal that we are doing more and give more than we can comfortably do or give. Or our anger may warn us that others are doing too much for us, at the expense of our own competence and growth. Just as physical pain tells us to take our hand off the hot stove, the pain of our anger preserves the integrity of our self. Our anger can motivate us to say "no" to the ways in which we are defined by others and "yes" to the dictates of our inner self.

—Harriet Lerner[1]

Through my journal, I reflect upon the amount of anger I have turned inward through guilt and shame. Responding with unhealthy anger to my daughters does not serve either them or me, and it builds a wall between us.

By about 10:30 a.m., my head begins to pound. It is getting progressively worse. Very quickly, it feels as though the voices of the other patients are too loud and are vibrating through my head. I consider, "Is this a result of anger from this morning and the incident with the tree, or am I having a migraine?" I have never had a migraine, although I have a few friends who do experience them. I try everything I can to breathe through it, but nothing works. I decide the best thing for me to do is go home, and I do. I sleep for two hours,

---

[1] Harriet Lerner, *The Dance of Anger*. HarperCollins Publishers, 2005

then wake feeling better after giving myself permission to relax.

The next morning, I share with my therapist the anger I had felt the day before over setting up the Christmas tree and tell her about the headache I had after. As well, I told her about the pain and the anger I have turned inward because of how I sometimes react with my daughters. I tell her how surprised I am at this realization, because I had never considered myself to be an angry person. She asks me to identify the most common times my anger toward my daughters surfaces, and we discuss the reality of each circumstance.

My younger daughter (who is now one and a half years old) is always on the go. I can't keep up with her, and at times, all I want is for her to be still and cuddle with me. When she doesn't comply, I become frustrated and respond with outbursts of anger.

The reality is that she is growing and is discovering new things. It is tough for her to sit still. That is *my* desire, not hers. I should embrace the moments in which she is still and wants to cuddle—and I should be grateful for them.

My older daughter (who is now five years old) has "attitude." She talks back, and we always have a struggle with her at mealtimes. I just want to throw her attitude right back in her face, and too often, I respond with anger.

The reality here is that she is going to have attitude and is going to act up—she is five years old. It isn't because I am a bad mom; it is simply the reality of the various stages of childhood. I must set healthy boundaries outlining how she may respond in healthy ways, and model healthy responses to her attitude.

My therapist gives me two homework assignments. One is to write three things for which to give myself credit as a mom, and the other is to keep a list of positive behaviors exhibited by the girls. To this list, I am to add the ways in which I have responded positively to their positive behaviors, and the healthy ways in which I have reacted to circumstances in which my anger begins to surface.

This afternoon, I go for my weekly massage only to discover that my usual massage therapist is away sick and that I have been scheduled to see another therapist, Nadine. The tension in my jaw and the headaches continue to be an issue, and nothing seems to help.

"I will have the tension in your jaw gone by Christmas," Nadine tells me, exuding a firm, gentle confidence that I had not felt from my regular masseuse. It isn't long before I recognize that Nadine knows more than just massage. I feel more connected and relaxed than I have in a very long time.

"It's obvious to me that you know more than massage. What else are you doing?" I ask her, genuinely interested in knowing.

"I am doing a combination of massage, acupressure, and Reiki on you right now. You have a great deal of suppressed emotion that is manifesting in your body," she tells me gently as she continues to work her magic.

I wonder, *How could she know about the suppressed emotion, the anger I feel, the serious depth of the depression?* We agree that I will see her twice a week for the next two weeks; she assures me that the tension in my jaw and the headaches will be gone in that time. Before

LEE HORBACHEWSKI

I leave, she gives me some tips and some breathing exercises that will help me to embrace and move through my emotions. Given the anger I have been dealing with, she has given me a timely and synchronistic message.

Resilience

> The strongest oak of the forest is not the one that is protected from the storm and hidden from the sun. It's the one that stands in the open where it is compelled to struggle for its existence against the winds and rains and the scorching sun.
>
> —Napoleon Hill

This morning, Wednesday, December 15, 2004, our session consists of listening to the instructors talk about resilience. I am grateful for this because the old tape of "I am stupid" comes up for me as they talk. I do not really understand the true meaning of resilience and so I sit, listening quietly and intently, taking in all they are saying. All at once I realize that I have, in fact, displayed incredible resilience throughout this journey. I reflect inwardly and celebrate myself for how far I have come and the courage it has taken me to be resilient and to step through the darkness and isolation. I *am* resilient. Resilience is the human capacity to face, to overcome, to be strengthened by, and even to be transformed by adversity.

In one exercise, we create a resilience map that allows us to recognize the factors that decrease and increase resilience. Shared in this way, it is so easy for me to see the areas and decisions in my life, particularly in the past year, that have sent me spiraling down into depression. Increasing resilience versus decreasing resilience shows me how I can choose to step through difficult times. Now that I understand what resilience is, I can see as I write how I have already developed resilience.

As I create my resilience map, I see various ways that I can commit to incorporating it into my life through creativity, time for myself, grounding, social activity, exercise, and healthful eating. Then a voice pops into my head: *You know all this stuff, but you won't do it. You are weak, and you will just continue to fall into your old habits of not taking care of yourself!* An uneasy feeling is in the pit of my stomach, and my chest begins to pound.

Lee, breathe; you are strong and have the courage to do anything you put your mind to, the quiet strong voice assures me.

I breathe and realize that this is the quiet voice of resilience, silencing the negative self-talk with positive self-talk. All along, this has been my voice of resilience, courage, being in the now, and developing positive beliefs. I wonder if this is what they mean when they talk about spirituality. Is this my voice of intuition and reason? A gentle smile comes across my face, a smile of knowing and of peace. Yes. It is.

MAINTAINING RESILIENCE

Facilitators: Chris &

What is Resilience?   Resilience Map!

Bath
Volleyball
yoga
PAINT
DECOORING
CREATIVE
YOGA
MEDITATION
GROUNDING
Use Colours
be creative

Time
For
me
RESILIENCE
Volleyball
MR. classes
Parties

work
out
EXERCISE
SOCIAL
Volleyball
Tae Bo

Social Activity vs Isolation

Support System vs not reaching out for support

Developing Positive belief vs negative beliefs

Positive self-talk vs negative self-talks

Realistic expectations vs unrealistic expectations

Aware of physical-tension/distress vs ignoring it

Good nutrition vs poor nutrition

Exercise & relaxation time vs lack of relaxation & exercise

Focus on present vs focus on past negative experiences or future worrying

My notes for the resilience map circa December 15, 2004.

Connection

When we get too caught up in the busyness of the world, we lose connection with one another—and ourselves.

—Jack Kornfield

Through all of this, I am realizing quickly how important and what a key role connection to self and to others is in ensuring my mental health. I see the coping skills behind which I have hidden. Isolating myself, withdrawing from others, and hiding behind a mask does not serve anyone, and it especially does not serve *me.*

Connection really is at the heart of life, of being truly healthy and authentic. On numerous occasions, I have witnessed the fact that when I express myself honestly I receive empathy, acceptance, freedom, and peace, all of which serve me in a positive way. The voice of fear and doubt pops up: *What if someone gets upset and turns their back on me or walks away?*

The quiet strong voice says, *Lee, when you come from a place of honesty and love, you can rest assured that those who matter will not walk away.*

I make a commitment to myself: moving forward I will be open and honest with myself and others, while honoring boundaries and being aware.

A simple autobiography that we are given as a handout touches me, it is the short poem by Portia Nelson "Autobiography in Five Short Chapters." As I read the poem, I am taken by the simplicity and profound truth in its message about walking down a street, and choosing a different path around a deep hole in the sidewalk, over the course of five days. I wonder. How many times do I do the same thing over and over again? How many times do I see something, yet choose to ignore it? How many times do I blame others instead of taking responsibility for my actions?

I am taken by the simplicity and the profound truth of this poem. I wonder, How many times do I do the same thing over and over again? How many times do I see something, yet choose to ignore it? How many times do I blame others instead of taking responsibility for my actions?

I return to my emotional health plan and examine my support network. Of the eight people I have listed, I ask, "Am I absolutely honest and as connected as I think I am?" In a moment of truth, I realize that there is not one person on my list with whom I am fully honest, open, and vulnerable. There is a theme to why I hold back with all of them: my fear of hurting them; my desire to protect their feelings; and my fear that they will leave, reject, or judge me. I question, "Is living in fear really a way to live life?" It holds me back from the real connection that I crave and need so deeply.

Then I realize that there is one person with whom I have been honest about every detail, from my childhood until the present: my therapist. In three short weeks, she has provided for me a safe space in which to reveal myself completely. I consider, Why is this? How can it be that I can open myself to a complete stranger? She now knows more about me than anyone in my life, including Neil.

I discuss this with her and ask her how I can have this type of candor in my relationships outside this program. "You have no past or future attachment to me," she explains. "The fears of judgment, abandonment, and rejection are not here. You are allowing yourself to be fully open with me, and I am here to listen and to support without judgment—that is my job. Once you let go of your fears and learn to trust in yourself and the people you love and who love you, you will find your relationships deepen and reach a whole new level when you are open and honest. Building an open and honest relationship takes work and commitment. We have had the opportunity to talk every day, and there is the commitment to your mental health that counts on that."

Her gentleness, compassion, and wisdom have taught me a great deal. I feel a twinge of pain as I realize our time together is coming to an end. This relationship with her has played a very important role in my ability to move forward.

At home, after the voice of doubt and the quiet strong voice go back and forth inside my mind, I lie in bed with Neil and talk to him about what my therapist and I discussed today. Through tears, I apologize to him for not being completely honest with him, for not letting him in. I share with him my fear of hurting him, my desire to protect him, and my fear that he will leave me. Neil holds me in his arms, listening closely and with unconditional love and acceptance. I know that the pain he has had to withstand on this journey has been difficult for him. He speaks very few words, which briefly causes me some discomfort, until he reassures me that all is well. I feel safe and loved, and I fall into a blissful sleep.

What I Know Now That I Didn't Know Then

- It's important to take time to heal with patience, grace, and love.

- I need to embrace imperfection and give myself permission to make mistakes.

- Don't assume how another person feels. I need to ask questions to clarify.

- Boundaries are a healthy way to maintain my mental health.

- Sharing with honesty and authenticity creates deep connection.

- Asking for help is a sign of strength.

- I am resilient and strong.

- I want to be honest and true to myself and others.

- I need to take responsibility for my choices and actions.

Chapter 5

Back to Reality

What lies behind us and what lies before us are small matters compared to what lies within us.

—Ralph Waldo Emerson

For almost two months, I have spent my life at the hospital. It has become a normal part of my life, and now it is coming to an end. I feel a mixture of emotions: relief, sadness, fear, loss, and gratitude. I feel the deepest gratitude for my therapist who has taught me so much, listened with an open heart and an open mind, and shown me compassion and caring. Mixed with my gratitude is a deep sadness, knowing that it is likely I will never see her again. I write a poem for her and give it to her on our last day. She is visibly moved and touched. In a small way, I have given back to her something for all that she has given me.

During our last session, we talk about moving forward; about my fears, goals, and relationships; and how I can continue on the path of self-discovery and knowing. It is a bittersweet time. I feel sincerely that this woman has changed the course of my life, and I will be grateful to her forever for the gifts she has given me.

Even though I am still very thin, weighing only one hundred twenty pounds, I am feeling much stronger physically. The day program has provided me with tools that make me feel equipped to move back into the reality of day-to-day life without further hospitalization.

Just as she promised, the most recent session with Nadine results in my jaw being relieved of the unbearable tension; as well, my headaches are fewer and less severe.

As Christmas eve approaches, my stomach becomes queasy. This will be the first occasion since I became ill that the entire family will be together. I wonder what they will all say, how they will react, whether I will have an anxiety attack, and whether it is too much for me all at once. All the worry and the "what ifs" fill my head with noise and clutter; my chest begins to pound.

Lee, stop! Pause and breathe; tell Neil how you are feeling and set healthy boundaries, the quiet strong voice advises.

As I share with Neil how I feel, I am aware that as he questions me and tells me I am being silly, he feels frustrated. I am taken aback. *Silly? You think I am being silly?* I say to myself as I feel anger rising within me. My first instinct is to withdraw and retreat, but instead, I find the courage to speak my truth.

"Neil, I feel that you are disregarding my feelings when you tell me I am being silly," I say, remaining calm and remembering the tools I learned for stepping through anger. "These are real fears for me. I am sharing them with you openly and honestly, and I feel as though you have just shut me down." I feel myself moving into a state of defensiveness. This is not healthy, and I know it.

As I have done many times in the past, I stand up and walk away, anger boiling within me. Neil becomes frustrated and snaps back, "There you go again, walking away." This does not help.

After a while, we sit down to talk again, both realizing that we responded to each other in ways that are unhealthy. Neil reassures me that if at any time during the evening I feel uncomfortable or overwhelmed, we may leave. Just knowing that he has acknowledged my feelings and has given me an alternative provides me with relief and with a sense of support.

Christmas Eve dinner comes and goes with very little mention of, or attention to, what I have been through. It helps that Christmas is a time of peace and joy, and watching the girls open their gifts brings me tremendous happiness. As I watch them, I remember my own childhood and how it felt to open gifts and to be fully in the moment, playing, giggling, and loving. As I visualize being in my Nan's house in Yamba, Australia, on Christmas Day, I feel a shift occur within me: I see the young carefree girl, filled with excitement and joy, lit by a smile from ear to ear as I opened each present.

As I connect fully to this moment in time, I feel every emotion in the depths of my soul. I smile that same ear-to-ear smile right here, right now. As I come back to the present, I look at my girls and see that same excitement and joy on their faces. They are so beautiful and filled with such innocence. I wonder when I lost that sense of wonder that came from the simplest things.

I discover something this morning that continues through the day as I play and connect freely with my daughters. The sense of wonder from the simplest things is right here in front of me and inside of me; I simply must allow it. For what seems to be the first time in a long time, I surrender to play and to being childlike and free, and experiencing the full joy of this moment.

Learning to Be Open, Honest, and Vulnerable

As 2005 looms, I make a New Year's resolution to play, connect, and be honest. I feel a renewed zest for life, yet, I am still aware of the boundaries I must keep in order to maintain my well-being. With my older daughter back in school and my younger daughter back to spending two days a week at Marie's, I choose to use the time alone in a loving and intentional way. I remain committed to my journaling and meditation, and I begin to research alternative ways to sustain my mental health.

I am surprised to learn from Neil that since I missed the November session of the Connections Retreat because I was in the hospital, they generously agreed to give me a spot for their next retreat in February. Not knowing too much about what to expect at this retreat, I have some fear about it. However, I open myself to the possibilities of further learning and personal development as I remember fondly my interaction with the compassionate Wayne last September.

It is February 23, 2005, and I arrive at the hotel where the Connections Retreat will be held. I am looking forward to a weekend away and to focusing on myself, so I choose to pay the extra money to have a room to myself. I don't really know what this weekend is about, and I have learned to cherish and to make the most of the time I have to myself. I admit that a few times over the weekend, as I witness the connections evolve between roommates, I have doubts that taking a room to myself was wise.

I learn quickly that the weekend is about authenticity and being open and honest within a safe, nurturing, and supportive environment. Though I have worked hard at finding and developing my inner strength, my physical body is still gaunt and weak. With a fear of the unknown, I participate quietly.

The first exercise we do is similar to one we did in the outpatient day program: each of us looks into the eyes of another person without saying a word. My prior experience with boundaries and with making assumptions when I was paired with the short woman came flooding back, so I applied what I had learned: look into my partner's eyes, be fully present and engaged. It amazes me how deeply I can connect with someone simply by looking into the depths of their soul through their eyes. *The eyes are the windows to our souls,* I think to myself.

We conclude the Friday night session with another reminder that I am not alone, that we are not alone. No matter how painful our life experiences, it is more than likely that others have walked through similar experiences too. Sharing our experiences is a meaningful way of connecting more deeply with others, and it is an opportunity I have not had before.

At one point, a question is asked: "Have you ever been raped?" and I stand in answer, then sit back down, feeling sick to my stomach. *Lee, you are such a liar!* I say to myself.

Lee, you can be open and honest, the quiet strong voice replies calmly.

I also am aware that as I hear some gut-wrenching, painful stories, I begin to withdraw, believing that my pain is nothing compared to that of others. With perfect timing, Terry, the facilitator, says, "There are no levels of pain. *All* pain is pain."

I lie in my bed after this session and write in my journal. I reflect on the rape story I have told myself for nearly twenty years, actually believing the story to be true. When I was seventeen years old, I was engaged to a man who I thought was the love of my life. When I discovered that he had been seeing my best friend for nearly a year, my dream came crashing down around me. In desperation, I made up a story that I had been raped when I was fourteen, and for a while it worked. His pity for me kept him by my side for a little while longer. Fortunately, as I saw in hindsight, the relationship was not to be and we parted ways, painfully. I used the same story with two other people: two boyfriends, when I felt desperate or I needed to fill a need for attention.

It is Saturday morning, and I know what I have to do. "I need to be open and honest with everyone." I stood up in our morning group, sharing, "I lied in the game last night. I stood to say I was raped, and the truth is I was not." I continued to tell the group about the story I had invented and had come to believe as true.

I was shocked by the response. Rather than being ostracized or judged, I was given acceptance, gratitude, and unbelievable support from the entire group for the courage I had shown in admitting my lie. I felt free of the lie.

Lee, with truth comes freedom! the quiet strong voice tells me.

It is Saturday evening, and I am brought back forcefully to my typical "giving until it hurts" mentality and not asking for help. For me, the most difficult game of the retreat is about giving and receiving. In uncontrollable tears, I find it hard to ask for help and to receive anything. Yet through this game, I am reminded of the lesson that my therapist in the outpatient day program taught me: "Asking for help is a sign of strength."

Returning to my room, I am overwhelmed with emotions. I journal everything I learned today: forgiveness, negative labels I have given myself, setting boundaries, and standing up for myself. I am also cognizant of the fact that many of the games we play are similar to lessons I learned while I was in the hospital. Now I am more open and in a better state of mind to receive and absorb these powerful, life-changing lessons.

It is Sunday, and I am given a taste of what it is like to receive unconditionally and without asking. I don't think I have ever cried as much in one day; this gives me another insight into how difficult it is for me to receive. Hearing, through the gift of their words, what people see in me, touches my heart deeply.

Now it is Sunday evening, and I am home sharing with Neil some of the experiences I have had over the weekend. I am a little taken aback because he doesn't seem to understand some of what I am telling him. I lie next to him in bed, looking into his eyes and wanting to connect without speaking.

"What are you doing?" he asks, looking at me as though I am from another planet.

"I want to connect deeply with you, sweetie, and to feel a connection that is beyond any words," I say, feeling a little disappointed that I need to explain it to him.

We continue to talk about my experiences at the retreat. I share with him the darkest secret I faced on the weekend, the lie about being raped. Neil was one of the boyfriends to whom I told the story. At the retreat, I had felt tremendous shame, guilt, and self-hatred that I had lied about it for so long when there were people there who actually had been raped. Admitting the lie to myself and to the other participants had freed me; yet telling Neil, the man I love deeply, that I lied to him requires another level of courage. It is difficult for me to share this painful lie with absolute honesty, allowing myself to be vulnerable to whatever reaction Neil has. True to the extraordinary man I am blessed to have as my husband, he embraces me and forgives me; we never speak of it again.

> "Then you will know the truth, and the truth will set you free."
>
> (John 8:32),
> New International Version

What I Know Now That I Didn't Know Then

- I need to approach conflict, anger, or fear from a place of love.

- I need to be aware of emotional coping skills: withdrawal, avoidance, and defensiveness.

- I need to embrace and love my inner child.

- I need to be present and grateful for the simple things.

- Giving is receiving, and receiving is giving.

- The eyes are the window to the soul. I can connect with people by looking into their eyes and being present.

- Pain is pain. There are no levels or degrees of pain.

- The truth shall set me free.

Chapter 6

Living Life

God grant me the serenity to accept the things
I cannot change, courage to change the things
I can, and wisdom to know the difference.

—Serenity Prayer

Present Tense

Over the next three years, I continued to participate in all the programs that the Inside Out Leadership Development Group (IOL) provided. I learned many lifelong lessons that I continue to apply to my life on a daily basis. Eventually I became a volunteer and cofacilitator with IOL. I found that people experiencing mental illness or having suicidal thoughts were drawn to me or perhaps I was drawn to them. At any rate, these interactions gave me my first insight into the path I was to follow. Terry proved to be one of the most powerful mentors and teachers I had, empowering me to accept *me*. Although I am no longer playing an active role in the IOL community, I am to this day eternally grateful for the community, for the treasured friendships I made, and for the lessons I learned through my involvement with IOL.

As my passion for personal development and self-discovery grew, I was fortunate to learn from many fantastic organizations such as Tony Robbins International. There, I spent six months with an amazing coach and decided to train as a coach myself, through Erickson College. I learned invaluable lessons and tools from the likes of Dan Millman, Jack Canfield, Lisa Nichols, Dr. Wayne Dyer, Louise L. Hay, among many others. I believe firmly that ongoing learning and continual development of self-awareness are key to remaining connected to my mental health and well-being. Also, I embrace the belief that we must always have a beginner's mind: approach everything with the eyes of a beginner and be open to learning.

Continually I embrace and learn that, "I am Becoming Resilient, Accepting, Vulnerable, and Empowered (BRAVE) while walking courageously through depression and anxiety." It is important to remember that I am *becoming*; it is not something at which I have arrived. I will never arrive because it is an unfolding journey.

Today I am grateful for my journey through depression, anxiety, and attempted suicide. It has helped me to connect with myself in a deeper way. I live my life authentically and realize that my life will always present me with challenges—it is up to me how I respond to those challenges. The lessons I have learned, and that I continue to learn, have created a powerful foundation for the person I am at my core: a being of love and light.

Between the publishing of the first edition of this book in May 2012, and now, I have traveled down the road of depression and suicidal ideation. In August 2012, I lost myself. I came dangerously close to ending my life at a time when, from an external perspective, everything seemed dreamlike. A false sense of success had engulfed me. I was riding the wave of ego and lost sight of me. Falling back into people-pleasing tendencies and stretching myself too thin, I reached a breaking point. The threads became unraveled—anger, resentment, blame, guilt, not honoring boundaries, and realizations of a change in how my support system looked.

I have discovered that now more than ever the quiet strong voice is the whisper of my soul—a soul yearning to be still. I am finding peace and comfort in my own being and listening to my own voice of knowing.

As much as I detest depression at times, it always presents me with yet more gifts of learning. For as long as I can remember, I have believed that there is always a positive aspect to every negative situation; however, sometimes it takes longer and is more difficult to see.

I am not perfect; I make mistakes. With integrity, grace, and authenticity, I continue to learn from each purposeful life lesson that comes my way.

> I am not perfect; I have learned to perfectly manage my imperfections.
>
> —Lisa Nichols

Depression is, and may always be, something I must live with—or perhaps it isn't. I have accepted that I may need to take antidepressants for the rest of my life—or perhaps I won't. It is with gratitude that I accept my situation, and yet I know that depression is not who I am and it does not define me. I have come to realize that depression is a gift that presents itself to me when I am not taking care of myself. All that I have learned from this journey helps me pass through each episode with more grace and understanding. I choose to stand on top of my story, not behind it, with the hope that others will be inspired to do the same.

Now I have come to a new chapter in my life: a time of change, letting go, and being present. It is a time of finding peace in stillness and joy in my own company, and of putting me and my family first. My daughters are now thirteen and nine years of age, a time where both are journeying through personal growth and finding their way. Now more than ever, the gift I can give them is that of a role model of healthy choices. I am grateful that I have the choice to stand beside them and be fully present to this stage of their lives. Ultimately, I wish to instill in them, and to all I know, the values of kindness, compassion, generosity, and gratitude in every aspect of life—the light and the dark.

Change always comes bearing gifts.

—Price Pritchett

I treasure the gifts change brings: the opportunity to grow, learn, and accept. The past nine years have presented me with a great deal of change, and change becomes easier to manage as I learn more about myself. And yes, change *does* come bearing gifts, although they may not always be the gifts you expect.

Chapter 7

Your Personal Reflection

With everything that has happened to you, you
can either feel sorry for yourself or treat what
has happened as a gift. Everything is either an
opportunity to grow or an obstacle to keep
you from growing. You get to choose.

—Dr. Wayne Dyer

No matter where you are in life, *awareness*, *acceptance*,
and *action* will help you to recognize, in any situation,
the importance of working through the truth, letting go
and surrendering, and taking conscious and intentional
action. I have tested this process time and time again. I
can tell where I have been in denial, when I stepped into
awareness, when I accepted the situation bravely, and
when I took courageous steps to change.

In 2004, I was not aware of these stages. I believe
that had I been aware of them, my journey may have
unfolded differently.

Today, and for the past couple of years, I recognize
that my awareness of these steps has helped me

85

tremendously with *all* of life's challenges, and especially when I have had bouts of depression.

When I am speaking to groups, I illustrate these stages through an example that is common to all of us: **time and the apparent lack of it**. For example, *I don't have time to connect with my friends and my family as much as I would like.*

Awareness	The truth is I *am* in control of how I spend my time. My family and friends are important to me. I need to find a way to make this work.
Acceptance	There are commitments I have: business, recreation, school activities, etc. Letting go of the negative perception that I have no time will help me to create space to be with family and friends.
Action	Arrange a monthly get-together—say, a regular Skype chat with long-distance friends and family—ensuring that I let my friends and family know how important it is to me to spend time with them.

Now let's apply these steps to **depression**. For example, *I am not myself and haven't been for some time. My moods are all over the place. I am having trouble sleeping. My eating patterns are irregular. I cry for no apparent reason. I feel isolated and helpless.*

Awareness The truth is I am not too sure what is wrong with me. I need help.

Acceptance I am sick. I must trust in others to support and help me through this. I must surrender to what I need and allow others to help me.

Action Today I am going to book an appointment with my doctor and/ or reach out to someone I trust and let them know, honestly, how I am feeling.

Facts

I am sharing this information with you so that you will know you are not alone. Depression is a disease that has an impact on millions of people across the globe. These are people who have experienced or who are experiencing just what you are experiencing. When I was in the early stages of deep depression, before I knew what it was, I felt as though I was the only person on the planet who was "crazy." (I no longer use that term seriously; I like to use it now in the context of "having fun.")

According to The Substance Abuse and Mental Health Services Administration (SAMHSA), a January 2012 national report reveals that

- 45.9 million American adults aged 18 or older, or 20 percent of this age group, experienced mental illness in the past year.

- The rate of mental illness was more than twice as high among those aged 18 to 25 (29.9 percent) than among those aged 50 and older (14.3 percent).

- Adult women were also more likely than men to have experienced mental illness in the past year (23 percent versus 16.8).

The report, *Quick Facts on Mental Illness & Addiction in Canada*, published by the Mood Disorders Society of Canada states

- There are 1 in 5 chances of having a mental illness in your lifetime in Canada.

- The percentage of people who commit suicide who have a diagnosable mental illness is 90 percent.

- There are approximately 4,000 suicides in Canada every year.

- Suicide accounts for 24 percent of all deaths among Canadians aged 15 to 24 and 16 percent of all deaths for the age group 25 to 44.

- Someone commits suicide every 40 seconds all over the world.

Warning Signs

Be aware of the signs. To this day, I am acutely aware of and understand the signs that focus my awareness on my mental health. It is important to be gentle and accepting as you acknowledge these signs.

Depression

According to the Canadian Mental Health Association, depression becomes an illness, or clinical depression, when the feelings and signs are severe, last for several weeks, and begin to interfere with one's work and social life. Depressive illness can change the way a person thinks and behaves, and how his/her body functions.

Symptoms include:

Sleep

- sleeping more or less than usual
- interrupted sleep—waking constantly throughout the night

Feelings and emotions

- feeling worthless, helpless, or hopeless
- crying for no apparent reason
- no feelings—lack of emotion toward others and yourself
- overwhelming sadness
- mood swings—one minute high, the next minute low
- difficulty concentrating and making decisions
- feeling isolated, alone, and rejected
- thoughts of suicide or death

Behaviors

- Withdrawing from family, friends, or regular activities

- Self-harm: cutting, scratching, and pulling out hair

Physical

- change in eating habits—sudden weight gain or loss; loss of appetite
- lack of energy; fatigue
- decreased sex drive
- lack of interest in physical appearance

One of the most useful tools I have found for finding the warning signs of depression is online at Depression Hurts (www.depressionhurts.ca). It has a free symptoms checklist that you may complete and provide to your doctor.

Anxiety

According to the Mood Disorders Society of Canada, while everyone feels anxious in response to specific events, individuals with anxiety disorder have excessive and unrealistic feelings that interfere with their lives, their relationships, their school and work performance, their social activities and recreation. The essential feature of the panic attack is a discrete period of intense fear or discomfort that is accompanied by at least four of thirteen physical symptoms, such as:

- palpitations, increased heart rate, or pounding heart
- sweating
- trembling or shaking
- sensations of shortness of breath or smothering

- feeling of choking
- chest pain or discomfort
- nausea or abdominal distress
- dizziness, unsteadiness, light-headedness, or fainting
- derealization or depersonalization
- fear of losing control or of going crazy
- fear of dying
- paresthesias
- chills or hot flashes

Personal Reflection

I invite you to find a quiet place to reflect, sit, and be open and honest with yourself. Have your journal or some paper with you and answer truthfully the questions I pose just below. If you feel it will be easier for you to have someone with you, then call a friend and ask him or her to come and do this exercise with you.

What is one thing in your life that is presenting you with a challenge right now? Focus on only one thing. Remember to take baby steps. There is no magic pill we can take to solve all of life's challenges at once. Start small.

Awareness: The Truth

What are you denying or pretending not to know?

_____

_____

What is holding you back from acknowledging the truth?

_____

_____

What is your fear about acknowledging the truth?

_____

_____

How can you take one step to move past this fear?

_____

_____

To whom can you reach out to receive support?

_____

_____

What affirmation can you say to yourself to remind you?

_____

_____

Does anything else come up for you in this moment?

_____

_____

Acceptance: Surrender and Let Go

How can you accept the truth and detach from the outcome?

_____

_____

How will this freedom make you feel? (Visualize how it would feel to let go of the fear, worry, stress, etc.)

_____

_____

What characteristics/personality traits do you need to embrace so you are able to move forward?

_____

_____

Who can you reach out to for support?

_____

_____

What affirmation can you say to yourself to remind you?

_____

_____

Does anything else come up for you in this moment?

_____

_____

Action: Conscious and Intentional Action

What are the steps you need to take? (These may be from baby steps to massive action. Remember, you may start as small as choosing to live one minute at a time.)

_____

_____

What does the final result look and feel like? (Visualize how it will feel; notice who you are being and what character traits you are displaying. Make note of *all* of these.)

_____

_____

What may hold you back?

_____

_____

How will you move past this?

_____

_____

When will you take these steps?

_____

_____

Who can you reach out to for support?

_____

_____

What affirmation can you say to yourself to remind you?

_____

_____

Does anything else come up for you in this moment?

_____

_____

Stand Up for Yourself: Creating Healthy Boundaries

The first step to creating healthy boundaries is to look at what you value. Values are who you are right now and who you are throughout time. They are the main beliefs that you hold to be of great worth in your life, and they are intrinsic to you as a human being. Knowing and recognizing what you value can help you with setting healthy boundaries by simply asking, "Does this align with my values?"

What do you consider to be values to you (e.g., family, generosity, creativity)?

_____

_____

_____

Now begin to list them in order of importance.

1. _____

2. _____

3. _____

4. _____

5. _____

6. _____

What choices are you making that honor you?

_____

_____

What is not working in your life?

_____

_____

How can you set a healthy boundary around this?

_____

_____

Does anything else come up for you in this moment?

_____

_____

_____

Speak Up and Ask for Help: Creating Your Emotional Health Plan

Who can you surround yourself with to support you at any given time? Your emotional health plan will help you in knowing who to reach out to and from whom to ask for help.

Outlining Your Emotional Health Plan

How to outline your health plan: Find a quiet place for reflection with a notepad and pen for at least thirty minutes. If time is a challenge, break it down into ten-minute intervals. Ask yourself the following questions:

1. Who is your support team—the people in your life who provide you with unconditional love, honesty, and support?

    Consider people in your life who are honest with you and have your best interest in mind. Make sure you have a mix of personal and business support. Write down the names of at least three people—preferably six!

2. What are the signs that let you know when you are struggling?

The key here is awareness. When you are aware of the signs your body is showing you, it is much easier to respond in a proactive and healthy way.

Do you

- experience physical signs (e.g., a burning sensation in your chest, headaches, numbness, tingling)?
- experience a change in your eating patterns (e.g., overeating, bingeing, skipping meals, cravings)?
- experience a change in your sleep patterns (e.g., interrupted sleep, insomnia, sleeping more than usual)?

3. What are the things you can do for yourself to find peace and calm? Knowing what to do without having to think gives you clear steps to manage your emotions.

What are the

- physical activities that help you (e.g., exercise, going outside for a walk, hiking, yoga)?
- relaxation methods you can use (e.g., meditation, listening to music, reading, writing)?
- positive outlets that you can surround yourself with (e.g., people, positive sayings, quotes, or mantras)?

Setting Up Your Emotional Health Plan

Phone the people you have listed for your support team and explain to them that you are setting up a plan to help and support you in challenging times. Tell them

- how you would reach out for help when needed (e.g., an email, a phone call, a text message).
- what you need from them (e.g., honesty, friendship, acceptance, a kick in the butt, accountability, a listening ear).

Once they have said yes, note all their contact information. (Be sure to add this into all your contact systems: email, phone, home address book, etc.)

Think about the format of your emotional health plan. What is the best way for you to display it? Is it in a word processor document, a spreadsheet, a colorful poster you create? Create something that will speak to you. You will find an example on the following page.

Be aware of the times you need to put your plan into action for both personal and business reasons, e.g., stress, financial worry, anxiety, challenges with children, challenges with relationships, etc.

Putting Your Emotional Health Plan into Action

Some of the most effective plans miss a key step—*action!* Be aware of two very important points:

1. What will help you to remain aware and to take action with this plan (e.g., reviewing it, having visual reminders (location), practicing it)?

2. What might hinder you from using this plan (e.g., lack of commitment to yourself, ego, complacency, fear)?

Emotional Health Plan Example

24-Hour Crisis Number: _____

Important Numbers

Emergency: _____

Doctor: _____

Therapist: _____

Support Team

Name	Home #	Cell #	Email
_____	_____	_____	_____
_____	_____	_____	_____
_____	_____	_____	_____
_____	_____	_____	_____

Tools for Peace and Calm

_____

_____

_____

My Mantra

_____

Show Up with Kindness, Love, and Gratitude: Embracing All Emotions

No matter what the emotion, you can choose to react in a kind, loving way and be grateful. This always starts with *you*.

How do you look for the good in yourself?

_____

_____

How do you look for the good in others?

_____

_____

What are ways that you can be kind, loving, and grateful to yourself?

_____

_____

What are ways that you can be kind, loving, and grateful to others?

_____

_____

What are three things you can do each day to show up with kindness, love, and gratitude?

1. _____

2. _____

3. _____

Does anything else come up for you in this moment?

_____

_____

_____

I congratulate you, and I am grateful that you have invested in yourself the love, grace, patience, and time to ensure your emotional well-being. My hope and my prayer for you is that you find your quiet strong voice to guide and nurture you and that you will find peace, joy, and happiness. Please remember: You are not alone, and you are loved.

Chapter 8

Supporting a Loved One

It is more than likely that if you know someone suffering from depression, you are watching helplessly as your loved one spirals downward into a world you do not comprehend. The signs may be subtle or you may see drastic changes; it may be that your intuition tells you something is not right. Follow your intuition.

Do not hesitate to ask your loved one how he or she is doing. Following is a guide that will help you to support your loved one. It is important to understand and be aware that most people who are suffering from a mental illness crave love, acceptance, compassion, and to be acknowledged and heard. These are what I craved when I was ill.

The first thing you must realize in supporting your loved one is that it is not about you. You must not take personally any actions or lack of actions on the part of your loved one. Always approach your loved one with kindness, love, and compassion; accept where your loved one is in the present moment.

There are several deeply hurting and damaging things one may say to someone with depression. I urge you to avoid saying these things:

- Just snap out of it.
- Don't be so dramatic.
- Why don't you just get over it, already?
- You have so much going for you, so wake up.
- Can't you just be happy?
- It can't be all that bad.

Be aware that your unhealthy reactions result from your own fears. Possibly you feel there is nothing you can do to help, no matter what you try. You may be frustrated because you cannot understand why your loved one is depressed. Perhaps you feel angry as you observe the impact your loved one's illness is having on others. Do your best to step past your own fears. Recognize that this illness is not about you and that your loved one needs your support, your acceptance, and most of all, your unconditional love. Meet your loved one where he or she is right now; do not try to change or to fix him or her. Depression is an insidious disease that carries far too much stigma and judgment already. You can alleviate that stigma and judgment for your loved one by educating yourself about depression and by being fully present to and accepting of your loved one.

Your loved one may not be able to give you a straight answer about what is wrong, but by asking the questions, you are showing that you care. More than likely, he or she is feeling alone, desperate, isolated, frustrated, overwhelmed, and helpless. Your unconditional and loving support will not cure the depression, but it will let him or her know that you are present and that you do care. Be aware that you may need to ask the questions more than once before you will get a response; there is a great deal of fear that arises when one admits that something is wrong and feels judged. Be patient and kind.

Here are sample scripts to use when asking.

- I have noticed you're not yourself lately. I am here to listen. How can I help you?
- Is everything okay? I am worried about you and want you to know I am here for you.

I like to use the acronym SUPPORT.

Seeking professional help

Unconditional love, acceptance, and compassion

Practice active listening

Praise

Overcoming being overwhelmed

Receive

Team

Seeking Professional Help

Going to a doctor or even calling a crisis line can be a daunting task for people dealing with depression. Having someone accompany them and support them may lessen their fears.

Here are sample scripts to use in approaching your loved one.

- I'm so grateful that you are sharing this with me. Let's contact your doctor and set up an appointment. I will happily join you in discovering how we can get you the help you need.

- As soon as we hang up, please contact your doctor and set up an appointment. I will call you back in an hour and check with you about when it will be. I'd be honored to drive you to the appointment. If you'd like, I will be present with you.

Unconditional Love, Acceptance, and Compassion

Judgment is one of the major and most damaging aspects of the stigma surrounding mental illness. Most people who are dealing with mental illness will not be open about it for fear of being judged or ridiculed. The biggest gifts you can give your loved one are your unconditional love, acceptance of their current situation, and the compassion they need and deserve.

Practice Active Listening

Allow your loved one to share with you how they are feeling and to speak without being interrupted.

- Listen with full attention and with the intention of supporting him or her unconditionally. Remove distractions such as television, radio, phone, and computer.

- Maintain open body language: face the person in a relaxed and casual posture. You may also "mirror" your loved one's body language—if he or she is bent over, face in hands, you can do the same. It is a sympathetic stance and will encourage openness.

- Maintain gentle eye contact; look into his or her eyes and connect at a soul level.

Praise

Celebrate positive steps. What to you may seem like small praise may go a long way for your loved one. Feeling trapped in a stream of negative emotions is common with mental illness. Gently point out any and all positive steps or emotions you notice.

Overcoming Being Overwhelmed

The simplest of tasks will more than likely result in your loved one feeling overwhelmed. Even mundane tasks such as eating or taking a shower may seem daunting. Receiving too much information at one time or too much support may also be daunting and may cause withdrawal. Keep things short, sweet, and simple. If you are in doubt, *ask them what works best for them.*

Receive

As a caregiver, you need support too. Be willing to ask for help and be receptive when others give you the support you need. Always honor your loved one's privacy; ask permission before sharing with anyone else what he or she is going through.

Team

You are one person. In reality, it is impossible for you to be the sole provider of support for your loved one. Instead, encourage your loved one to create an emotional health plan and appoint a support team. An example of this is at the end of the previous chapter. This team consists of trustworthy friends and/or family who have the best interests of the person in mind and heart; the most effective team will be a mix of personal and professional support.

This too shall pass. Your acceptance and *support* of your loved one will help him or her heal. You will become more knowledgeable and understanding of depression.

Thank you for being present with your love. Without the support team I had during my depression, it is unlikely I would be here today.

Chapter 9

Resources and Help

24-Hour Crisis Support Lines

North America: 1-800-SUICIDE (784-2433)

Australia: 13 11 14

UK: 08457 90 90 90

Republic of Ireland: 1850 60 90 90

Crisis Line listings across the world:
www.iasp.info

Global Resources

International Association for Suicide Prevention (IASP)

www.iasp.info

IASP is dedicated to

- preventing suicidal behavior

- alleviating the effects of suicidal behavior
- providing a forum for academics, mental health professionals, crisis workers, volunteers, and suicide survivors

World Health Organization (WHO)

www.who.int/topics/depression/en/

WHO is the directing and coordinating authority for health within the United Nations. It is responsible for providing leadership on global health matters, shaping the health research agenda, setting norms and standards, articulating evidence-based policy options, providing technical support to countries, and monitoring and assessing health trends.

Befrienders International

www.befrienders.org

The aim of the global network, Befrienders Worldwide, is to encourage the development of effective support services, and by sharing information and working together, improve our ability to

- ensure maximum access for callers to appropriate emotional support services
- demonstrate effective service policy and practice
- share information
- offer mutual support
- influence policy both internally and externally

Canadian Resources

Mood Disorders Society of Canada (MDSC)

www.mooddisorderscanada.ca

The MDSC was formally launched and incorporated in 2001 with the overall objective of providing people with mood disorders a strong, cohesive voice at the national level to improve access to treatment, inform research, and shape program development and government policies with the goal of improving the quality of life for people affected by mood disorders.

Canadian Mental Health Association (CMHA)

www.cmha.ca

The CMHA, founded in 1918, is one of the oldest voluntary organizations in Canada. Each year it provides direct service to more than 100,000 Canadians through the combined efforts of more than 10,000 volunteers and staff across Canada in over 135 communities. As a nationwide, voluntary organization, the CMHA promotes the mental health of all and supports the resilience and recovery of people experiencing mental illness. The CMHA accomplishes this mission through advocacy, education, research, and service.

Canadian Association for Suicide Prevention (CASP)

www.suicideprevention.ca

CASP was incorporated in 1985 by a group of professionals who saw the need to provide information and resources to communities to reduce the suicide rate and minimize the harmful consequences of suicidal behavior.

US Resources

National Alliance on Mental Illness (NAMI)

www.nami.org

From its inception in 1979, NAMI has been dedicated to improving the lives of individuals and families affected by mental illness. NAMI advocates for access to services, treatment, supports, and research. NAMI is steadfast in its commitment to raising awareness and building a community of hope for all those in need.

National Institute of Mental Health (NIMH)

www.nimh.nih.gov

The mission of NIMH is to transform the understanding and treatment of mental illnesses through basic and clinical research, paving the way for prevention, recovery, and cure.

Australian Resources

Beyond Blue

www.beyondblue.org.au

1 300 22 4636

Their mission is to create national focus and community leadership to increase the capacity of the broader Australian community to prevent depression and to respond effectively. Their aim is to build a society that understands and responds to the personal and social impact of depression, and works actively to prevent it that improves the quality of life for everyone affected.

Mental Illness Fellowship of Australia Inc. (MIFA)

www.mifa.org.au

MIFA is a national network of service providers with members in every state and territory, working alongside individuals and families affected by serious mental illness.

UK Resources

Mind

www.mind.org.uk

Mind is both a local and a national network. This organization works with approximately 250,000 people every year. They are able to help people who experience all types of mental distress and who may require help from one or more of our services. They demand higher standards in mental health care and challenge discrimination wherever it occurs.

Rethink Mental Illness

www.rethink.org

Rethink Mental Illness is a charity that believes a better life is possible for the millions of people affected by mental illness. Today they support almost sixty thousand people every year across England as they get through crises, live independently, and realize that they are not alone.

Internet Resources

- American Psychological Association: www.apa.org
- British Columbia Schizophrenic Society: www.bcss.org
- Canadian Association for Suicide Prevention: www.suicideprevention.ca
- Headspace: www.headspace.org.au
- HealthyPlace.com: www.healthyplace.com
- Kids Help Phone: www.kidshelpphone.ca
- Mental Health Commission of Canada: www.mentalhealthcommission.ca
- Postpartum Support International: www.postpartum.net
- Postpartum Progress: www.postpartumprogress.org
- PsychCentral.com: www.psychcentral.com
- Reach Out: www.reachout.com
- The Balanced Mind: www.thebalancedmind.org
- The Bipolar Burble: www.natashatracy.com

Books That Have Inspired Me

Over the course of the past several years, I have found great inspiration and comfort in many books. These books have touched my heart in profound ways. Each of these books listed below represented a powerful shift in my attitude and mental health.

A special thank-you to Dan Millman, Pema Chodron, Oriah Mountain Dreamer, Dr. Wayne W. Dyer, Byron Katie, and Neale Donald Walsch, whose books and messages in particular have made a significant impact on my life.

- Beck, Martha. *Steering by Starlight*. Rodale Inc., 2008.
- Brown, Brene. *I Thought It Was Just Me (But It Isn't)*. Gotham, 2007.
- Brown, Brene. *The Gifts of Imperfection*. Hazelden, 2010.
- Chodron, Pema. *Start Where You Are, A Guide to Compassionate Living*. Shamghala Publications, 1994.
- Chodron, Pema. *The Wisdom of No Escape, and the Path of Loving-kindness*. Element, 1991.
- Covey, Stephen R. *The 7 Habits of Highly Effective People*. Fireside, 1990.
- Dyer, Wayne W. *Change Your Thoughts–Change Your Life*. Hay House, 2007.
- Dyer, Wayne W. *The Shift*. Hay House, 2010.
- Ford, Debbie. *The Right Questions*. Harper Collins, 2003.
- Hay, Louise L. *You Can Heal Your Life*. Hay House, 1999.
- Holden, Robert. *Be Happy*. Hay House, 2009.

- Katie, Byron. *Loving What Is*. Three Rivers Press, 2002.

- Millman, Dan. *The Journeys of Socrates*. Harper Collins Publishers, 2006.

- Millman, Dan. *The Life You Were Born to Live, A Guide to Finding Your Life Purpose*. H. J. Kramer, 1993.

- Millman, Dan. *The Way of the Peaceful Warrior*. H. J. Kramer, 1980.

- Myss, Caroline. *Invisible Acts of Power*. Free Press, 2006.

- Nichols, Lisa. *No Matter What*. Wellness Central, 2009.

- Oriah Mountain Dreamer. *The Invitation*. Harper Collins, 1999.

- Oriah Mountain Dreamer. *The Dance*. Harper Collins, 2001.

- Oriah Mountain Dreamer. *The Call*. Harper Collins, 2006.

- Osho. *Awareness, The Key to Living in Balance*. St. Martin's Press, 2001.

- Ruiz, Don Miguel. *The Four Agreements*. Amber-Allen Publishing, 1997.

- Shimoff, Marci. *Happy for No Reason*. Free Press, 2008.

- Walsch, Neale Donald. *Conversations with God*. Putnam, 1995.

Books Specific to Mental Health

These books have been a source of inspiration, resources, and exercises that I have used for myself and in supporting others. Many have given me a deep understanding and further knowledge of how the brain and the mind work.

- Ackerman, Diane. *A Slender Thread: Rediscovering Hope at the Heart of Crisis*. Vintage, 1998.

- Bennett, Shoshana S., and Pec Indman. *Beyond the Blues: A Guide to Understanding and Treating Prenatal and Postpartum Depression*. Moodswings Press, 2003.

- Blauner, Susan Rose. *How I Stayed Alive When My Brain Was Trying to Kill Me*. Harper Collins, 2002.

- Brantley, Jeffrey. *Calming your Anxious Mind*. New Harbinger Publications, 2007.

- Dockett, Lauren. *The Deepest Blue*. New Harbinger Publications, 2001.

- Goleman, Daniel. *Emotional Intelligence*. Bantam Dell, 1995.

- Hawkins, David R. *Power vs Force: The Hidden Determinants of Human Behavior*. Hay House, 2002.

- Leahy, Robert L. *Beat the Blues: Before They Beat You*. Hay House, 2010.

- Lerner, Rokelle. *Living in the Comfort Zone*. HCI, 1995.

- Lipton, Bruce H. *The Biology of Belief*. Hay House, 2008.

- Shields, Brooke. *Down Came the Rain*. Hyperion, 2005.

- Southerland, Mary. *Hope in the Midst of Depression.* Harvest House Publishers, 2007.

- Williams, Mark, John Teasdale, Zindel Segal, and Jon Kabat-Zinn. *The Mindful Way through Depression.* The Guildford Press, 2007.

Gratitude

This healing journey has been filled with support, friendship, and love from many people. During the darkest times, family and friends were there, even through their own discomfort and fears.

My husband, Neil, was and is my foundation and my rock. He held our family together in the most difficult times. He gave me the space to heal and the loyalty of his unconditional love.

My beautiful daughters have taught me many lessons. They've tested me and filled my life with love and joy. They are my number one teachers.

Mum and Dad, for bringing me into the world, for your sacrifices and unconditional love, thank you.

All my family, by blood and by marriage, who have been there in so many ways, I could write a whole chapter thanking each of you.

To my emotional support team that has evolved over the years: Leslie, Catherine, Natalie, Kim, Gisele, Val, Heather, Corrie, Kate, Tina, Elizabeth, Lynne, Kari, Farhana, Natasja, Tessa, Francie, Susanne, Gemma and Jo. I am so grateful for all of you.

To the therapists and mental health professionals who have had a long-lasting impact on my life, my thanks.

To my family doctor, who has supervised and worked closely with me on monitoring my medication.

Many people have been a huge source of support, direction and resource for publishing this book. Thank you to Susanne Alexander-Heaton, Farhana Dhalla, Charmaine Hammond, and Annette Stanwick for your wealth of wisdom and support.

Thank you to Yvonne Basten for your editing help.

To Robin for your help with the publishing logo, designing and printing the initial promotional materials.

Thank you to Tanis for your initial editing and for your honesty.

To Tina, for your encouragement and for being the first person to read the first draft of my book, you have my gratitude.

To everyone who read the original manuscript and provided feedback, comments, and testimonials, I appreciate you and your comments.

Terry Lige and the IOL community, who gave me a safe and loving community to heal and grow, thank you.

To Dan Millman, for helping me find my peaceful warrior, and for your humble wisdom.

To Oriah House, who has quietly inspired me through her authenticity, kindness, and support with re-writing the Introduction.

To Lisa Nichols for encouraging me to share my story.

Thank you to Gemma Stone for your touching foreword, inspiration, and support.

LEE HORBACHEWSKI

Thank you to the Distress Centre in Calgary, the entire team, especially Michelle, Roxanne, and the volunteer who answered the phone.

Sandra, your friendship meant the world to me. In your passing, I have felt you in my presence, lovingly guiding and supporting me.

About the Author

Lee Horbachewski has delivered her message of courage, hope and inspiration as a speaker to thousands of people. Although not currently practicing, Lee is a certified professional coach through Erickson College International. Through her personal experience and many of the people she has worked with, she believes the *number one* step in starting the healing journey is to feel heard, loved, and accepted—beginning with self. She is a quiet strong voice of hope, inspiration, and

people impacted by mental
and and two daughters in

.mpLeeSerene.com